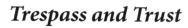

Trespass and Trust

Trespass and Trust

QUAKER MEETINGS AND SEX OFFENDERS

Daphne Glazer

 Quaker Books

First published in May 2004 by Quaker Books
Friends House, Euston Road, London NW1 2BJ

ISBN 0 85245 356 6

Cover design by Jonathan Sargent

Typeset by Andrew Lindesay at the Golden Cockerel Press
Printed by Biddles

Copy editing and appendices by Anne Hosking, with preparatory work
by Seren Wildwood

We are grateful to Frankie Rickford and Stacey McNutt for advice in
the preparation of this book

Contents

Foreword
Beth Allen

"What does it mean to live in the Light?"

Through several years of discussion of child sexual abuse, both among Quakers and in British society, this is the central question that has surfaced for me.

This is not simply an abstract question. The 'inward Light' is the potential for goodness and integrity in each human being. This is a central Quaker principle. It is as Friends in the Light, Friends of Truth, as Quakers in the Religious Society of Friends that we meet for worship, for witness, service and caring.

In various ways, a considerable number of Friends have had personal experience of dealing with sexual abuse and its repercussions. Quaker meetings* have given thought to the safety of children and young people at Quaker events, and in our regular children's meetings, summer camps and national gatherings. During this past decade, Friends have caught a vision of the potential for restorative justice and the enlightening power of friendship which we and others can give to ex-offenders. And many of us – more than we know – bring slowly into the light of consciousness the fact that we are the survivors of some sort of abuse, whether as children or as adults. For some this uncovering of earlier abuse is acutely, even unbearably painful; others, while disturbed by it in childhood, have now integrated it into themselves and live with it like an old scar. And I know of several meetings and a number of individual Quakers who have brought into the light of public knowledge the fact that some of us have

---

* 'Meeting' is the word that Quakers use for gathering together in worship; it also the name used for events, activities and groups, the equivalent of church or congregation. Among themselves, Quakers refer to each other as 'Friend', the two words are interchangeable.

convictions for child abuse. I have sat with Quakers as they talked about how Friends were shocked at what they had done, how their meeting would not accept them and how, although they had come to acknowledge it as part of themselves and resolved never to abuse again, this change in themselves had not been recognised by those with whom they met in worship.

The promptings of love and truth in our hearts bring us, however reluctantly, to realise that we are living in the Light of God with all this painful knowledge. Can bringing what we know (whether in general or in particular) into the Light be part of our shared healing?

As the General Secretary of Quaker Home Service from 1990 to 2000, I felt that we needed to put down some of the Quaker experience which had been gathered at considerable cost. I was also mindful of our staff, for whom Friends, as employers, must provide clear procedures and criteria to work with. After consulting with colleagues in Quaker Peace & Social Witness I decided that we needed a book that would enable us to gain from our collective knowledge, not deny it. I wanted to know that the experience, insights and sheer hard work of all those involved in bringing this issue into the Light has been worth something.

I have seen the Light at work in:

- The experience of survivors of abuse
- The experience of people who have offended
- The passion of parents for their children's right development
- The deep searching of meetings and event organisers as they seek to make open and obvious their concern for children's well-being
- The professional thinking of Friends in prison and social work
- The work of staff in establishing good and safe foundations for our children's and young people's meetings
- The desire to build trusting communities

This forms a considerable body of Quaker experience to learn from. Underlying it all I was aware of Quaker principles which could help us to work with the disturbing knowledge we were bringing into the Light. What I needed was someone who could talk with all these people, listen to their stories, gather all the experience together and write it down. Daphne Glazer is a Quaker, a prison minister (chaplain) and a published author who has worked with her own children's meeting. She agreed to do the job.

All those she talked with knew of her project and their part in it. All gave consent for the words and insights to be quoted. Apart from published books or public documents from Quaker meetings, they are quoted anonymously, so that the confidentiality of the interviews can be respected.

Quaker thinking is based on experience. It is based not just what we ourselves have been through individually in our own minds and bodies, but on our shared experience as corporate groups, as meetings. And within the bodies of our meetings we bring different experiences together, some hard to hear about. If our corporate thinking is to be whole, healed and fully developed, we need to hear from each other, to bring into the Light the shadows and the achievements, the stories of failure and the stories of survival, even of victory. For it is a victory when powerless children or adult victims support and empower each other, when they tell their stories of abuse first to each other and then to those in authority, when they become survivors and begin the long healing process.

Sexual abuse is an issue of power rather than sex. Quakers can be ambivalent about power, in our own communities and in the wider society. We may criticise its misuse and claim to 'speak truth to power' on behalf of the oppressed, yet we often deny our own power as a body of predominantly middle-class, comparatively rich people in a dominant Western nation. No wonder our thinking and feeling about the misuse of power is so often confused.

In this book Daphne helps some of us, powerless and powerful, to tell our stories. She gives us some of the facts, and outlines the Quaker insights and testimonies we can bring to our thinking and decision making. Here, too, is some of the story of Britain Yearly Meeting and the central work on this issue: here is the contribution of the Quaker organisation in these islands towards good thinking and good practice. I thank Daphne Glazer for this book and I thank also all who have contributed to it.

Trespass and Trust is both a collection of people's stories and a reflective book. It is not a practical handbook, though it does include some guidelines developed by some meetings and appendices with resources lists. In it some survivors speak about the damage done by abuse, and the resources lists refer readers to several Quaker and other publications about safeguarding, and about the care of victims. Their accounts suggest some helpful ways that Friends could respond to a survivor, and again the appendices indicate how listeners could learn more. However, there are comparatively few books published about sex-offenders in a community: this is the first Quaker book to focus, as far as we know, on how a meeting might seek the Inward Light in an offender, to keep the vulnerable safe while accepting him into the worshipping community.

We hope that *Trespass and Trust* will help meetings to handle difficult situations without causing further damage. Perhaps, too, we can think through some of the tough questions about forgiveness, suffering and evil by considering real events which some of us have lived with, rather than abstract hypothetical ones. And all of us can learn the value of praying for everyone caught up in stories like these, as we discover for ourselves the Light at work in the silent depth of worship.

A note from the editors

This book contains no explicit descriptions of sexual offences. Nevertheless it does not make easy reading.

As you read it, please bear in mind that many of those who have contributed their stories did not find it easy to tell. Daphne did not find it easy to write, and those who have worked on the manuscript since the first draft have often struggled too. Each of us has faced the content as an individual, as well as bringing our professional skills to the task.

We hope that the book may at least represent one more stop along an inevitably hard road, and that readers will find in it not only challenges but glimpses of hope.

Taking care of yourself

Please start your reading of this book as Quaker staff start each discussion of this subject, with a reminder about our need and our right to take care of ourselves.

Be aware that, in considering the issue of sexual abuse, feelings or memories may arise and disturb. If this happens, please look after yourself, as you explore the disturbance or as you recover from it. You do not have to be alone.

Ask for prayerful support: you do not need to explain why. You could talk to someone you trust: some meetings have appointed someone with the special gift of listening well as an overseer for survivors. You can find the contact details of the Quaker Women Survivors of Childhood Sexual Abuse among the organisations in the appendixes, where helpful publications are also listed.

You live in the Light, and the Light of love lives in you.

Introduction

Daphne Glazer

One afternoon I received a surprise telephone call. How would I feel about researching and writing something about sexual offending as it affects Friends and meetings in Britain Yearly Meeting? Beth Allen, Helen Drewery and Sue Baker, all members of Friends House staff and involved respectively with child protection, the Circles of Support and Accountability, and Quaker prison ministry, had been discussing the need for a publication which would help meetings cope with issues of sexual abuse, and in particular help them to respond safely and with care to a former prisoner wanting to worship with Friends.

In the beginning I was reluctant to embark on this task – sexual offending by its very nature seemed an intractable matter and I think I probably wanted to avoid considering its implications, so I hesitated before I accepted the challenge. Perhaps one of the main reasons for my reluctance has been the fact that periodically I have worked with groups of teenagers on writing workshops in drop-in centres, and in a women's centre, at which I have encountered people who have suffered sexual abuse from their families. I have seen the effects of such traumatic events on them and have been harrowed myself. The question I was dodging was: could I bear to know what might be revealed?

The idea of speaking with people about some of their most painful moments; of having so much trust placed in me and bearing the responsibility all this entails were other considerations which I couldn't avoid.

Initially I had no idea where my researching might lead and, before embarking on it, I read several booklets produced by the Church of England and some work in progress by the Methodist Church regarding the sex offender issue. These began to give me an idea of the complexity of what was involved.

From my meetings with Beth, Helen, and Sue, I understood something of the need for a publication which would stand alongside *Meeting Safety** but be of a different nature. *Meeting Safety* is the handbook for children's and young people's meetings, and is about all aspects of safe working, including protecting the vulnerable from abuse. *Trespass and trust* should explore the effects of sexual abuse on survivors and perpetrators, in particular exploring the relationship between meetings and offenders. The book would attempt to consider what concrete proposals meetings have made in order to cope with situations where an ex-offender might present himself or herself at a Quaker meeting.

Over and above all this book would look at how we may use our experience and insights as Quakers to help bring the issues raised into the light.

Although this book was intended originally for Quakers as the worshipping group, other churches and faith groups may be interested to see how we are dealing with this difficult problem. The views of all faith groups will surely be of great value in helping us to create a more humane and just society.

As this subject is so intricate and as we as Friends are such very varied people, I have tried to give a flavour of the great multiplicity of views and feelings of all members and attenders – to do more would perhaps be impossible because of the very nature of our Society. I have done my best to represent the voices of many of those who felt able to speak out, and I feel very grateful to them for venturing into this painful territory and for trusting me. For survivors of abuse this has been often a very harrowing matter – I have had long evening conversations on the telephone, often with people who preferred to remain anonymous – and I have for a few moments been privileged to gaze into the abyss of their grief. I have also shared exhilarating and triumphant times, when people have spoken of their ways of overcoming

---

*Details of *Meeting Safety* and all other publications quoted in this book can be found in the Appendix 3 on page 88.

hurt. Their accounts make clear why we must have the courage and honesty to ask ourselves: how would we greet an ex-offender in our meeting?

For many who have for years kept silent about the sexual abuse which they have suffered, the opportunity to express their feelings in a publication, has, so they tell me, come as a release.

Fifty-seven people either wrote in or telephoned me to speak of their own experiences or to share their views. In some cases this happened in response to a letter in the weekly journal *The Friend* asking for information; at other times it was in reply to a phone call from me, to people with whom Beth and Helen had previously been in touch. Others gave up their free time to attend meetings with me.

I have talked too with ex-offenders and have been heartened by their honesty and their determination to change. Gradually over months all these personal stories began to show me the direction of the book. They fitted alongside the words of social workers , those working in criminal justice, the insights of elders (responsible for the spiritual life of the meeting) and overseers (who offer pastoral care to all in the worshipping group), and all who have helped to draw up guidelines for meetings in the forming of a framework to ensure that they can offer a true sense of emotional security to worshipping groups.

I am really sorry that I have been unable to use all the contributions sent in, one or two even from abroad, but it must be said that these have nevertheless contributed to the overall thinking on the matter.

I do thank everyone who has contacted me for their willingness to address a difficult subject. All were happy to have their contributions published, but it was agreed that all those used – unless previously published under the author's name – should remain anonymous. Meetings referred to have also not been named, unless we were quoting from a published document.

Anyone reading this may wonder who I am and why such a request would have been made to me. Two aspects of my life recommended me, I believe. For many years I have been connected with prisons – I have often thought that I am in some way inextricably bound up with them. Over twenty years before I was born, my father spent three years in Dartmoor Prison as a conscientious objector in World War I. As an adult I have come to realise that this had a profound effect on his life and on those of all of my immediate family. Most of my contemporaries' fathers fought in World War II. I carried the knowledge of this difference inside me from being a small child. I always knew that my family were set apart from those surrounding us – we lived in the 'spit and sawdust' end of Sheffield. Knowing that my own father had been in prison made me want to enter that world and see it for myself, so when the chance came I took it. Over thirty years ago I became a member of the Religious Society of Friends. A member of Hull meeting, Alec Horsley, ran a social studies group in Hull Prison, which I joined. This group gave me my first glimpse of prison life.

I was to teach in Hull Prison several years later, and subsequently in a Borstal for young offenders for a very brief period (I now give writing workshops at the Wolds private prison). Following this was a gap of some years before I again became caught up in prison life – this time as a Quaker Prison Minister on the chaplaincy team: I am still there.

Because of my contact with prisons I have found myself, as a writer, often using imprisonment and the lives of offenders as themes in short stories and now in a novel. At a recent Quaker Prison Ministers' conference at Woodbrooke Quaker Study Centre I read a story from one of my collections. Having heard this, Helen and Sue began to wonder whether I might be a suitable person to take on the project they and Beth had in mind.

So this is one strand, and through it I came to know Beth, Helen and Sue.

Throughout this, at times, very grim and painful journey, I have been helped and supported by some wonderful conversations with Beth Allen and Helen Drewery. Anne Hosking, Mina

Temple, and Sue Baker have also given me vital support. I feel I have learned a great deal throughout the writing and I am surer than I have ever been that there is 'that of God' in us all.

Acknowledgements

I would like to thank the following people for their help in creating this overview: Kate Cairns for her wise words on the phone and for sending me her book; Sheila Gatiss for clear vision and astute advice mediated over the telephone; Marian Liebmann for giving me an insight into 'restorative justice', so vital in this connection; Lesley Moreland for her wisdom and humanity; Sue and Bob Johnson for their pioneering, unafraid, and humane spirit; Tim Newell for 'telephone guidance'; Marian Partington for sharing the unspeakable and transforming it; 'O', who made a long journey to share difficult thoughts with me and hold these reflections in the Light.

There are many others whom I cannot list here for reasons of confidentiality, though I would like to say how deeply indebted I am to them all.

1
The Quaker Community

In any meeting for worship, strangers, long-standing members, visitors, newcomers and regular attenders, people known and people not yet known to the meeting may be worshipping together – yet even familiar figures contain the unknown and the unknowable. This can be a source of enrichment and interest, but it may also cause anxiety and fear.

The last thirty years have seen vast social changes both here and across the world, and these are often reflected in changing attitudes and a new openness about matters such as sexual abuse, which once tended to remain hidden. This of course is a positive development and ought to help bring about a safer and more just society. However the media (mainly the tabloid press) in this country has succeeded all too easily in enflaming public opinion and in creating a climate of hysteria and fear by its often sensationalised portrayal of cases involving abuse. This rather than solving problems has created new ones and obscured the real issues.

Friends tend to find ways of defusing conflict and calming frenzy. But perhaps to assist in some measure, it may be valuable to explore the present situation and see what we can learn from the experience of some meetings and reflect on where we stand in the light of Quaker teaching.

What are the issues?

Whenever a meeting is held, amongst those present there are likely to be those who are survivors of abusive relationships; their relatives; those whose close relatives, husbands, wives, partners have committed sexual offences; and children and other vulnerable people. It is also conceivable that there may be those who have in the past committed Schedule 1 or other offences or who in fact are still engaged in doing so. These are serious sexual offences listed in Schedule 1 of the Sexual Offenders Act 1997 for which registration with the police is required. The types of offences which under the Protection of Children Act 1999 attract disqualification from working with those under 18 years of age as part of the sentence include murder, culpable homicide, abduction, rape, offences of cruelty and assault, sexual abuse and offences relating to indecent behaviour and child pornography. The situation when a Schedule 1 Offender is involved in the Quaker community has the potential to be nightmare territory. On the other hand what is perhaps more likely is that the meeting has not had to encounter such a scenario yet. Instead, considering how to apply the guidelines in *Meeting Safety* has led Friends to wonder what the meeting might do, were such a situation to arise.

Faced with a real situation where the meeting must take steps to safeguard all its vulnerable members and set up a framework for its activities, the matter does in a sense become more straightforward. What is perhaps more difficult to deal with is a hypothetical situation, a 'what-if . . .'. One of the major problems for Friends in contemplating the message given in *Meeting Safety* is the refusal by some to accept that such safeguards are necessary. How can we comprehend sexual abuse?

Abusive behaviour can be habitual and hard to change: it can be usefully understood as a form of addiction. The slim volume, *Beyond my Control*, edited by Chris and Gil Skidmore, is very valuable in that it allows Friends to speak about addiction both in themselves and others, and how it has impinged on their lives. By so doing it brings things into the light, which tormented the individuals concerned, because they must remain silent about them. This book lets us see people as they are and not as we assume they are.

In *Grounded in God*[1] a life-long Quaker, brought up in a Quaker household, speaks of being sexually abused as a child by her controlling father and never daring to tell anyone about it. She asks Friends to believe that what she is saying is the truth: 'Realise that sexual abuse of children can happen, that Quakers aren't immune.' And finally: 'This openness can help Quakers get past the concept "not in our meeting" or "not in our town". It can help Friends to get past their need to believe that "that type of person just wouldn't do that". The article concludes with the telling sentence: 'Quakers need to remember that we're not perfect'.

The Society's reputation for integrity has a long history. George Fox's life preached honesty and straightforwardness in all things. Friends are still inspired by the words of George Fox, a founder of Quakerism, in 1656: 'Be patterns, be examples, in all countries, places, islands, nations, wherever you come, that your carriage and life may preach among all sorts of people, and to them; then you will come to walk cheerfully over the world, answering that of God in every one'.[2]

Under the heading 'honesty and integrity' in the index of *Quaker faith & practice* we find this challenge in the first chapter, commonly known as *Advices and qiiueries*: 'Are you honest and truthful in word and deed?'[3] We see this insistence on personal integrity in Friends' insistence on affirming in court rather than swear an oath. Our honesty should, we are gently reminded, pervade every aspect of our lives from personal relationships to business ones. This honesty means we do not hide from or deny difficult facts. The truth, when we face it, can make us free.

But over and above all this is our central belief in 'that of God' in each one of us; the seed of something divine, which if we nourish it, can transform our lives. When George Fox first propounded this testimony it was regarded by the authorities of the day as heretical. Since that time it has so permeated Friends' lives that it can cause us to be reluctant to admit that those around us may be committing or have committed an offence which has injured someone else; or that such a situation might arise. 'That of God' is a potential in each person, not a guarantee. Sometimes 'that of God' is hidden deep or denied.

The challenge for Friends to-day it would seem lies in retaining our idealism, whilst at the same time remaining vigilant and aware that we are all indeed capable of the heroic and the base, and in coming to terms with this essential human dichotomy.

Matters for Reflection

As an individual:

◆ *How do I feel about what I have just read? Can I talk to someone?*

As a group:

◆ *How prepared are we to deal with the issue of potential sexual abuse within our meetings?*

◆ *Are we able to look truthfully at our meetings?*

2
What Makes a Meeting?

In every meeting there will be those who have been Quakers all their lives, some who became members having been convinced as adults, and those who worship with Friends, attending without formal commitment. Sometimes those in membership are outnumbered by visitors and other attenders. Whereas in the past many members of the worshipping community would have come to the Society originally from other Christian groups, nowadays meetings are increasingly home to those with backgrounds in Judaism, Buddhism, Islam, other faiths or none.

Those who have been in membership for many years may find the changing face of Quakerism quite disturbing. Where there may well have been settled family units, now in the modern inner city meeting – or indeed in rural areas, too – there are often single parent families coping alone with the upbringing of children, others estranged from their family group and all in need of the meeting's support.

People new to Quakerism often come to meeting looking for a spiritual lead and sometimes are surprised at the lack of what they might consider 'clear guidelines' regarding our beliefs. Our beliefs are not set in stone but are rather revealed experientially over time in our lives and are constantly evolving and being tested.

The very nature of our beliefs, their lack of prescribed dogma and the insistence on personal commitment and responsibility attracts individualists. George Fox's words still challenge: 'But what canst thou say?'[4] This can be both a strength and a weakness. On the one hand it leads to innovation and daring; on the other to dissent and argument.

Friends often seem to have difficulty when they must deal with something which threatens to disturb the even tenor of the meeting. After all, we argue, Quakers have been at the forefront of the peace movement for a very long time, as we can see from Margaret Fell's words of reassurance to Charles II in 1660, 'We are a people that follow after those things that make for peace, love and unity; it is our desire that others' feet may walk in the same, and do deny and bear our testimony against all strife, and wars . . .'[5]

The stress we place on peace naturally makes us very reluctant to disturb the harmony and yet sometimes, for the sake of justice and true community, we must do so. We tend to forget also that early Friends were stormers and ragers against injustice, and were not afraid to voice their opinions. There is an at times narrow divide between being tolerant and being weak. Some, too, might mistake tolerance for weakness.

In the same way that Friends are sometimes unprepared to admit the negative potential of others, we may also try to dodge facing conflict. However, Friends should be uniquely placed for dealing with thorny matters because of long familiarity with the ways of conflict resolution. Many Friends are involved in projects such as 'restorative justice', and there are others of us with 'alternatives to violence' skills who may be called upon to help – Quaker Peace & Social Witness (on page 94) offers training. After all, these methods have been designed to foster community and help us relate to one another. Such skills have never been more important than in present times when traditional family units are fracturing and the international situation appears so bleak.

Usually in the event of some conflict arising in the meeting, those responsible for eldership (i.e. for the spiritual life of the meeting) and others appointed to oversee all those in the Quaker community (i.e. to offer pastoral care) tend to be the ones first called upon to mediate in difficult interpersonal relationships. *Conflict in Meetings*, one of the eldership and oversight handbooks, has a useful chapter exploring a number of areas which might test or divide a meeting on occasion.

3
Survivors' Stories

We have been assuming, so far, that certain sexual relationships are not about love but about power, and therefore destructive. Some people may argue that a particular relationship was exceptional, or that the law is wrongly applied. We need to check any assumptions against the experience of those who have been abused.

In every meeting there may be those who suffered some very traumatic happening in their lives, perhaps occasioned by an abusive relationship; or there may be others whose close relatives or friends have been injured by abuse.

In *Query 18*[6] we are asked whether we enter 'with tender sympathy into the joys and sorrows of each other's lives'. In order to do this we may find ourselves listening to stories which at times may be inordinately sad, perhaps almost unbearably so. If we fail to listen, those who have endured abuse may feel that they are being shunned because other people do not know how to respond to their suffering and are recoiling from it.

John Lampen in *Mending Hurts* says that 'in our private lives, too, we develop an armoury which defends us from the pain of others, specially when it takes forms which pass the hurt to us.' Writing of those who have suffered a trauma, 'the person who has been hurt by another loses some of the sense of human solidarity. We are reminded of our essential loneliness.'[7]

What do these survivors say to us? Can we hear them? Can we listen to their stories?

We have respected the confidentiality of individuals by using a letter of the alphabet, rather than inventing pseudonyms; changing or omitting recognisable details. Meetings have been given a roman numeral.

∗

One person, A, who attended a Quaker meeting, is a survivor of childhood abuse. She feels she can no longer attend meeting for worship (though the abuse was unconnected with Friends): she has problems with Quaker silent worship as she feels that Quaker 'silence' may be a refusal to face the truth. In silence she hears the echoes of her traumatic past where the abuse remained hidden because it was never acknowledged.

'I thought the idea of the silence was to listen within and discover if God spoke. Inside me there was only screaming. For me, learning to listen to the screaming has been the most positive outcome of trying to find silence.'

However, 'I never found much plain speaking in meeting. Instead silence was used to tackle issues or as a "let's wait until it goes away" tactic. My response to this is paradoxical because on the one hand pretending things do not exist was what I had grown up with, and on the other I thought and indeed expected to plain speak because that was what Quakers were about. That, of course was not how it worked out in reality.'

∗

As a small child B was abused by her father for eight years. She considers that 'there is more concern for the perpetrator rather than the victim'. She feels that Friends are more ready to get involved with international concerns than matters closer to home.

The horror of child sexual abuse in the family lies, she thinks, in the fact that the child's love and trust of its family has been betrayed. In order to survive the child freezes into forgetfulness. 'Women of my generation often haven't been well enough to face what has happened to them, but now it's coming out because we're old enough and well enough to remember . . . Some of the images I get, I'm looking down on myself – the images go away in a box. This has made me learn to compartmentalise my life.'

B sums up the situation: 'It takes great resilience and strength to be a victim.'

*

Another worshipper, C, was also abused in childhood by her father, who was an Anglican vicar, and she expresses similar sentiments: 'We are survivors and our trust has been damaged.'

She reflects that because of this early experience she became '. . . easy game. You are looking for love but you don't get it, and you can't give it.' She subsequently experienced a violent marriage, a marriage which looked on the outside to be quite stable but – as with her early abusive relationship with her father – nobody knew of the true situation. All remained hidden. 'We act strong, act leadership. Inside the child is still there.'

*

C, like B, also went through an out of body experience but she couldn't look at what was happening to her.

Of her traumatic past only perhaps one person in her Quaker meeting has any knowledge. 'You can't talk of this openly or people would see you as a figure of pity.' Of late C has been able to speak with others who have endured abusive relationships. 'It's like coming out, because you're a different species and you'll never feel like other people do.'

*

D has endured hardship of the most extreme nature: her father abused her from six to sixteen. He went on to murder one little girl and rape another, for which he received an indefinite prison sentence: 'The judge said he hoped my father would never be let out.'

At her father's trial it was revealed that he had abused her cousin and a lot of other children and he had had affairs with half the women in the road where they lived. She remembers as a child how glad she used to feel at her father's absence from home, during his repeated prison sentences – he was a petty thief.

What D could not understand at the time was why her mother appeared to be totally unaware of what was happening all around her. For a long time after she left home in her teens D did not want to have anything to do with her mother. Subsequently, she has felt differently about this relationship and realises that perhaps her mother had to blank out the horror because she couldn't cope with it.

The pain did not stop after her father's imprisonment because ten years later her brother, age twenty-six, committed suicide – he had been sixteen at the time of her father's trial and had been left to shoulder the grim news alone. She thinks he could not come to terms with what his father had done. There had of course been extensive press coverage of his father's case.

In more recent times D was to experience more heartache: 'I thought I'd coped quite well – then I discovered my daughter had been abused by her father.' D's daughter no longer speaks to her. For D it is as though she is experiencing in some way a re-run of the relationship she had with her own mother. 'I've learnt a lot,' says D, 'since she and I have been apart.' She feels that she did not dare to let herself get too close to her daughter because 'everybody else does.'

She says she has survived these many traumatic events through being something of a workaholic. 'All you can do is get on.'

D has been able to share some of this with some members of her meeting. She says she is of an age where she does not see any point in its concealment.

*

From another, E, comes a further story of abuse and concealment:

'I am rapidly approaching old age, a lifelong Friend, my
mother came from a long line of Quakers, my father was a convinced Friend [becoming involved as an adult]. My father abused
me when I was 11 and I was so ashamed that I never told anyone
until 12 years ago and only then because my sister told me he
had abused her too. What a mixture of relief and sadness, relief
because now I knew that it wasn't somehow my fault, and sadness
that she had had to go through it as well.

'The reason that I blamed myself was that he was such a good
person, a well-respected Friend. He died in the 1960s and even still
other Friends will say to me how much he meant to them.

'I went for counselling – my daughter arranged it for me with
a wonderful person – I was able to work through everything, but
then I was left with a father I hated. I went back again and was then
able to get to a stage where I had a father whom I could love for the
great Dad he was. Nevertheless I realised what he had done was
very wrong and adversely affected me for the majority of my life
not to mention the effect it all had on my husband and children.

'Although it still hurts to talk about all this, I feel that I am now a
whole person, which I certainly didn't feel before the counselling.

'Not all Friends know about this in my meeting. The first
people I told were also Samaritans and were very understanding
and supportive. I think that it is a particular Friend who can be of
help and not the meeting as a whole.

'What needs to be got across is that child sexual abusers are
not bad but what they do to children is bad – have they any idea
of the effect their abuse has?'

It would seem that for many women now in their fifties,
sixties and above the abuse which they suffered at the hands of
relatives and family friends has only now been revealed. Their
suffering over all those years of childhood and young adulthood
is something which we must deplore and it should strengthen us
in our resolve not to let to-day's children suffer a similar fate. For

the older women often the climate of the times in which they grew up will have been a factor in silencing their anguish.

*

A disabled Quaker, F, has suffered an even greater barrier to having her voice heard than those who are able-bodied. F says of her attempts to talk about her situation, 'I've said things but people don't listen – they're embarrassed because they find it strange. They are afraid of their own sexuality. My mother abused me – my father was fine and it was only when I grew up that I discovered that men could be different from my Dad. My mother was very dangerous. I was ill and I'm very handicapped. I was very bashed up because she wanted a son . . . He would give me things to do when I was strong enough. I had to stop my Mum doing things to my sister. In the end my mother went into a mental hospital.

'You have to be very courageous to cope – only the strong survive. I joined the Society thirty-two years ago. I believe in God, in the spirit – that helps me. I believe that God will turn things round.'

*

We should be careful not to assume that in the Quaker community – in any community – the vulnerable people will inevitably be female; men too may have been the victims of sexual abuse, about which they have always remained silent.

G wrote: 'In my teens I was sexually abused by a friend – an older married man for whom I had much respect. He was active in the same church where he was held in high esteem, having talents as an actor and artist . . . He had a sense of humour, which I too appreciated. His wife was a teacher . . . in a school where he helped. I was often invited as a friend. I am unsure what effect the abuse had on me.

'I was one of six children, four boys and two girls. We were rather poor and I had to sleep with an older brother, there too sexual abuse went on though on a more minor scale. But I imagine this happened in those days and was disregarded.

'I think of a far more serious nature – affecting me educationally and psychologically – was the state school I had to attend from years five to fourteen. I was in a perpetual state of fear from the sadistic attention of masters and mistresses, which caused my mental processes to black out. One example stands out. The class was asked to paint an object. I was given a nasturtium to paint. I was pleased with what I had been able to do. Then the headmaster came round and marked mine 4/10. He asked all boys who were marked less than 5/10 to stand up, and caned all of us. I have never felt confident enough to draw or paint since.

'But concerning the relevance of the effect of sexual behaviour on me, I believe the at times violent, sadistic attitude at school, and even by my mother, produced in me too great a preoccupation with that instead of the loving, understanding attitude which should prevail.'

*

Particularly upsetting too and cause for deep concern is the story of Joe Jefferey. The Testimony to the Grace of God in his life, presented to Britain Yearly Meeting in 2002, records that he gave great service to the wider society and to the Society of Friends. He died aged twenty, loved and grieved by many. 'Tragically, he was unable to share his own appalling experience of male rape. The consequences of having to carry this evil burden and the suffering it caused led to his ending his own life.'

*

From all these stories we can see that in many meetings there exists an often unmet need for us to really listen to one another and to try to see below the polite social surface, which may hide isolation and an unexpressed grief. We have to ask ourselves whether we dare meet this need. If we are reluctant to do so, we must consider honestly what the reason for our reluctance may be.

Abusive relationships thrive on secrecy. Tim Newell, former Governor of Grendon prison, is of the view – as are so many Friends working in the area of criminal justice – that we all have to behave in more transparent ways. Victims feel anger, rage and then guilt – sometimes feeling 'am I to blame, have I caused this?' People feel guilty about feeling angry because it is not socially acceptable to express anger by screaming and shouting out the pain. Victims are expected to subdue these feeling, but anger has to be valued and validated by others.

How can a meeting help victims reach towards healing, and honour those who can call themselves 'survivors'? One essential element would be the meeting's commitment to preventing abuse.

Matters for Reflection

♦ *How do people 'learn to know one another in the things which are eternal'?*

♦ *How ready are we to confront difficult interpersonal situations? By being conciliatory do we fail to face problems and work through them?*

♦ *Do we pray for all victims, whether known to us or not?*

4

Forgive us our trespasses as we forgive those who trespass against us

How do we cope with hurt? Does forgiveness heal? But how can we forgive? Who forgives? What is forgiveness? Is there a Quaker view of forgiveness?

A present day Friend, Jocelyn Burnell, whilst refusing to accept the idea of religious faith as an easy palliative, still believes that those who have suffered will be helped by God to bear their pain: 'Sometimes religion appears to be presented as offering easy cures for pain: have faith and God will mend your hurts; reach out to God and your woundedness will be healed. The Beatitude "Blessed are they who mourn, for they shall be comforted" can be interpreted this way too, but the Latin root of the word "comfort" means "with strength" rather than "at ease". The Beatitude is not promising to take away our pain; indeed the inference is that the pain will remain with us. It does promise that God will cherish us and our wound and help us draw a blessing from our distressed state.'[8]

The experience of forgiving

Friend B, who told us some of her story in the previous chapter, has discovered that because of her past life she has become passionate for justice and she is able to use this in her professional work. Recently she found the strength to meet her father, someone whom she had not seen for over thirty years and who was now an old man, walking with a stick. This was a profoundly strange and moving experience.

She said to him, 'I want different pictures of you in my head.'

As B looked at him, she could see how facially alike they were – their eyes are even the same colour- and she was appalled. Standing beside him she realised her strength as a survivor, and his past dominance shrank away; he was only a stooping old man, who could not accept his own guilt. But she has experienced the triumph of knowing that they were able to speak with each other in a civilised way for forty minutes.

✳

At the idea of someone who had abused others sexually being in meeting, D is not disturbed. She has worked as a Samaritan and has at times had to listen to people sobbing out stories of abuse they have committed. She thinks that she has been able to cope with things of this nature because 'My Dad admitted it – that is the crucial thing for me.' For victims of abuse in families an admission by the offenders of their guilt seems to be vital if they are going to heal.

✳

Two Quakers, who have both suffered the ultimate loss through murder, one of a sister and the other of a daughter, have written in detail about their journey through rage, pain and devastation towards forgiveness. By doing this, they have shown us their refusal to be ground down and destroyed by the experience; their courage is humbling. Can we trust George Fox's words? 'I saw that there was an ocean of darkness and death but I saw that there was an infinite ocean of Light and Life and Love that flowed over the darkness; in that I saw the infinite love of God.'[9]

Marian Partington's sister, Lucy, disappeared on December 27th, 1973 and not until twenty years later did Marian learn that she had been murdered by Frederick and Rosemary West. Her careful and courageous exploration of forgiveness is illuminating. She wrote in diary form of how she received this news:

'. . . Words must be found. There must be some thing for all of us to learn from this profoundly shocking profanity before it gets buried under the concrete of fear, prejudice or even worse, indifference . . . It is about my quest to find meaning by trying to remain open to the pain, the joy, the rage, the grief and what lies beyond. It is about the living with the reality of violence, rape, torture and murder, trying to face up to it and trying to transform it . . . It is about salvaging the sacred.'[10]

In Alison Leonard's book, *Living in Godless Times*, Marian says 'If you're going to forgive, I think you've got to get to the depth of the enormity that you're trying to forgive. Forgiveness in this case began with me experiencing murderous rage. I knew at that moment that I had the capacity to kill, which I chose not to carry out . . .

'What happened to Lucy has brought me up against the absolute need to find some method of reaching inner peace. The phrase "Be still and know that I am God" is important to me. Not that I like the word "God". But knowing God, then knowing myself; knowing that I have the capacity to murder, knowing that Rosemary West has the capacity to love.'[11]

Marian has strained to understand why the Wests acted as they did and she believes they had been brutalised by the sexual abuse they experienced in childhood, their actions were driven by powerlessness and rage. In the case of Rosemary West, Marian thought, she seemed to want to make her victims feel what she had felt.

A vital part of moving towards forgiveness lies in 'experiencing the grief deeply', after which she reached 'a deep state of peace, an experience of being human. I knew that everything was impermanent, and none of us is unconnected or separate. That is a silent place, like a Quaker meeting at its best, which embraces everything and allows for true compassion.'

*

Lesley Moreland also worked at forgiveness. In her book, *An Ordinary Murder*[12] she writes about the horror of learning that her daughter, Ruth, had been murdered (though not abused). Lesley's struggles to accept what had happened and to fight clear of victimhood are very poignantly portrayed.

Finally after the passage of some years, she did get to meet Ruth's killer, though at first he had refused to see her. She felt that she could not forgive him but she managed nevertheless to convey to him something of the agony which he had caused to so many people. All the time Lesley was wrestling with the enormity of what had happened, she was concerned with the idea of forgiveness. By the end of the book she had become convinced that only Ruth could forgive her murderer, and that it was not her mother's place to forgive.

Thinking about forgiveness

Tim Newell, in *Forgiving Justice*, says that forgiveness is no easier than repentance. Our rage at the person who has harmed us can drive us to seek revenge: 'Revenge however enslaves us and the spiral of vengeance seems woven into the fabric of social realities. There is a certain irreversibility about our actions, which makes it difficult to escape the mutual distrust. The only way through the predicament of irreversibility is through forgiveness.'[13]

We go back to the words in which Jesus showed us how to look at these issues in the confidence of God's presence and guiding light –

'Forgive us when we go wrong, help us to forgive those who wrong us.'

'Forgiving,' Tim Newell writes, 'is an intense personal experience in which feeling about the other person is central. It involves overcoming our feelings of resentment about the other, regaining our sense of worth and separating the action of the wrongdoer from their person.'

But this does not mean that forgiveness is a substitute for justice, a point that Marian Liebmann stresses. It is all very well to tell victims that it will do them good to forgive and that it is their Christian duty to do so, even when the aggressors have not asked to be forgiven! Justice and reparation must enter this equation.

In the book *Restorative Justice – what's it all about?*[14] she sets out the principles:

- Victim support and healing is a priority
- Offenders take responsibility for what they have done
- There is dialogue to achieve understanding
- There is an attempt to put right the harm done
- Offenders look at how to avoid future offending
- The community helps to reintegrate both victim and offender

By holding to these principles we are far more likely to help both the victim and the one who abused. The victim's hurt will have been acknowledged. The offender will have been able to own the responsibility for his or her crime, to apologise and offer reparation, and to reassess his or her future behaviour bearing this knowledge in mind.

Rupert Ross writes in *Returning to the Teachings: exploring aboriginal justice*, that 'Interconnectedness lies behind the justice system in its insistence that offenders should not be dealt with alone without the victims and all those "touched" by their behaviour.'[15]

Of course for Marian Partington too, as she wrestled with the trauma of loss, it was this sudden recognition of the connectedness of all things, which brought her healing and she knew that 'none of us is unconnected or separate'.

Women speak out

Bringing the Invisible into the Light[16] records how a group of women have struggled against feelings of impotence, loss and rage to reach peace of mind. Here emotions and feelings, which have remained hidden from view, have been triumphantly brought 'into the Light'.

Bringing the Invisible into the Light was a Swarthmore lecture, presented to over 1,000 British Quakers at Yearly Meeting in 1986. Up to that time many had not really thought about the things of which the Quaker Women's Group were speaking. In some cases they were appalled and there was a great deal of denial.

One of the pieces opens with these words: 'I had a violent childhood'.[17] The writer, J, was raped by her father, a very violent man, and grew up to be cowed. In order to distance herself from sexuality she entered a convent. Realising that this way of life was not for her, she eventually left the convent and later found Friends:

'They gave me permission, which I could not give myself, to reject the strait-jacket that Christianity was for me. They also showed me, through the Peace Testimony and the teachings of non-violent direct action, that other ways than those I knew, were possible.'

Another woman, K, a survivor of incest, has come through pain, suffering and rejection and is now able to say: 'One of the most sacred names for the divine is I AM. Now I recognise that I share the divine.'

In this book we have generally referred to abusers as 'he', and survivors and victims as 'she', because that is how it so often is. Though that is an issue for other books to consider in depth, we as Quakers need to ask ourselves how our Testimony to Equality relates to sexual abuse – which is not about love but about power.

For L the very maleness of much religious language has always been a burden. From her earliest childhood she noticed it. In adulthood she has finally reached the point where she can say: 'My spirit knows that God is not male and my intellect and experience show me only too painfully the results of that way of talking about God.' L challenges Friends to acknowledge the sexist nature of the language we use in worship.

'Healing,' wrote M, 'cannot come without pain and without going deep into that pain the wound cannot heal with a clean scar.

Instead there is only a healing over, leaving the pain to re-erupt at a later date.'

Hazel Shellens researched the effects of *Bringing the Invisible into the Light*, both the lecture and its companion book.[18] In the immediate aftermath of the lecture a huge amount of correspondence was generated. Some considered that *Bringing the Invisible into the Light* did not amount to a Swarthmore lecture, it did not have the status or weight. Women interviewed remember hearing the following repudiations: 'These women were lying, no one would have been raped within the Society . . .' 'They were not real Quakers – birthright Friends have not had such experiences.'[19]

At this point a number of Friends obviously found some of the issues dealt with in the lecture too painful to contemplate. Hazel Shellens quotes from an American Friend, Judy Brutz: '. . . even thinking about family violence among Friends is for many of us to enter an area of the unthinkable.'[20]

However the lecture was to open up a more realistic view of some areas of human behaviour as evidenced in the series of booklets dealing with sexual issues, which appeared after 1986. A group of Quakers concerned for the healing and prevention of sexual abuse brought out their booklet[21] relating to child abuse. The handbooks *Safeguarding Children from Harm*[22] and *Health, Safety and the Law*[23] now succeeded by *Meeting Safety*,[24] are all part of this venturing into dealing with aspects of human conduct, which many Friends have been very reluctant to acknowledge.

Even today though, with these positive developments in bringing abuse into the light, occasions do still arise when those in our meetings may suffer because their appeals for help go unheard or unrecognised. Take the situation which N encountered at a residential Britain Yearly Meeting recently, where an older man made a sexual approach to her. She did not get the chance to tell anyone about this at the time, and when she did seek help after the gathering she had the impression that her feelings were not being taken seriously by those in whom she confided. Then the following year, again at Yearly Meeting, another older man made a similar advance to her.

'I realised that he too was seeing me sexually. I was really upset. Was I doing something to attract this sort of thing? Was it unsafe to talk to strangers even at Yearly Meeting?'

However, after seeing an overseer N 'received the unexpected gift of an apology from two members of the man's meeting, who were aware of his tendency to button-hole young girls. This lifted my heart so much that I was able to take in my stride subsequent encounters with him. I felt safe again, doubly safe, because I had learnt both that I could protect myself and that others would pro-tect me . . . I now have personal experience of the difference it can make to feel that other people in a meeting know what is going on and to be supported by them in this kind of incident.'

This story illustrates clearly the need for us to be watchful and imaginative in safeguarding all who are associated with our meet-ings. If we do not listen or do not respond, we may cause deep hurt to others and fail them when they most need support.

Men, too

Male survivors may have the additional burden of battling against expectations of maleness, or assumptions that men are not victims, on their road to recovery. There is so much in our culture which stresses 'machismo'. *Out of the Shadows: help for men who have been sexually assaulted,* by Sarah Stott, though aimed specifically at men suffering from trauma caused by sexual abuse, contains much information that could also be helpful for women survivors. *Out of the Shadows* does however mention something in the section near the end dealing with aids to survival, which perhaps pertains more to men than women: men can and should 'forgive' themselves for being 'vulnerable'.

We are aware that the focus of this one short book, *Trespass and Trust,* has had to be narrow. In the Religious Society of Friends, as in the wider society, we need to hear from men who are survivors, too.

Matters for Reflection

- *What is the meeting's duty?*
- *How can we support vulnerable people in our meeting?*
- *In what ways do we foster an atmosphere in which Friends find they can talk about their needs? Can those who give care acknowledge their limitations?*

5

The Meeting's Responsibility

Paedophiles target vulnerable communities –single parent families, for example, and church communities. At its best a Quaker meeting is a community of friendship, where we can find God in our lives together. In friendship we trust each other, we grow, we learn from others whom we admire, we take on responsibilities, we take delight in each other's company. A Quaker meeting therefore, like any religious community, may be particularly attractive to a paedophile. The are good opportunities for intimacy with and authority over a young person or a child, opportunities which can be perverted. The trust that is the basis of a meeting can be destroyed. How can we make a meeting safe enough for each individual to be truly free? How can we be vigilant without destroying the very qualities that we value?

What can we say about child sexual abuse?[21] deals with the nature of such abuse, and its effects. There is too often a 'wall of silence' surrounding abuse and this causes 'barbed wire' round the child's emotions that can prevent access for help and support being given.

'The "barbed wire" image represents the emotional barrier round the inner self which keeps the person shut off, locked in by his or her inarticulate pain.

'In addition, the wider society has put up its own wall of silence. This is built of embarrassment and discomfort around emotional and sexual matters, pressure for conformity and respectability, and unenlightened stereotypes that fail to accept that it is the abuser who is the problem and not the child.'

Part of this booklet is concerned with ways in which healing may be brought about, but it finishes with the following words: 'Individual healing is not the final point of arrival for those whose concern is the sexual abuse of children: our aim is the healing of society. Without the courage of survivors during the last twenty years in this country, the silence might well have gone on. We are each responsible for teaching ourselves and others, and for protecting the vulnerable and offering love and support in healing ways.'

Indeed the protection of children and young people is the concern of the whole meeting and not simply of the small group directly responsible for looking after them while their parents are in meeting for worship.

Meeting safety

There is recent legislation that makes it possible to check whether those working with children and young people have relevant criminal records. Our own publication, *Meeting Safety*, describes good practice with, for example, the recommendation that at least two suitable adults should supervise children's groups. The complicated forms on which a volunteer applies for disclosure of his or her record, the need for enough people to supervise activities for children and young people, can make heavy demands and may lead to tensions within our meetings.

In the past the running of children's meeting and young people's groups was a much more informal – even casual – arrangement and Friends unused to the present level of safety measures sometimes feel that they are unnecessary. They may be reluctant to accept the need.

Kate Cairns, author of *Surviving Paedophilia*,[25] considers that the major problem is getting people to think about this: 'We aren't talking about a little problem, and we also know how rare a conviction is.'

Research suggests that between one in ten and one in twenty of the population has actually been harassed, raped or abused sexually. We must also bear in mind that according to current statistics there are over 70,000 on the Sex Offenders Register, and others convicted before the Register was established, or convicted of lesser sexual offences, or before changes in the law on homosexuality. The crimes vary. Amongst them will be those who have engaged in 'unlawful intercourse', for example sexual intercourse between a teenager of seventeen and one of fifteen, just under age. Nonetheless we do have to assume that there are quite a lot of people whose thinking and feeling around children is dangerously distorted.

Kate Cairns points out that we know very little about other people's experience of sex and sexuality, of whatever kind. We have to deal with our feelings whilst at the same time thinking clearly. Problems arise because feelings are so strong. The taboos regarding childhood are very powerful and this makes it very difficult to think clearly about the situation. We must try to think neither hysterically nor dismissively.

A further difficulty is that most abuse happens inside the family, and is carried out by family members or people trusted by the family, and by abusers who have themselves often been victims.

There are also predatory paedophiles who target the vulnerable – families with single parents, for example, or people who have been abused before. Church communities which place a high value on family life, on trust, openness, fellowship and interaction with people of all ages, are also vulnerable.

Someone who is very much involved in helping sexual offenders to overcome their offending behaviour is Donald Findlater of the Lucy Faithfull Foundation. In an interview, he stressed that we must all be aware of the fact that child sexual abuse may arise anywhere. 'I fear sometimes in faith communities there is a blindness . . . We can prevent child sexual abuse but only if we can see it and talk about it.' In Philadelphia, U.S.A., Donald has seen posters on public transport, drawing people's attention to the dangers of child abuse. He thinks we need this openness here, and he has helped bring the organisation *Stop it now!* to the UK.

Amongst the people whom he treated between seventy and eighty percent had been sexually abused themselves. 'Children are sexually assaulted by people who have responsibility for them. They are not usually sexually assaulted by a predator. But the predator is a person too and there is a danger in the use of labels that we dehumanise people.'

It is clear, then, that those who are going to lead children's and young people's groups need to be above all trustworthy where children are concerned. The selection of such people demands great tact and has to be dealt with in a loving manner. It is also very important to take up their references and check criminal records.[26] Probably only a person with a deep knowledge of individuals in a meeting can serve with discernment on the nominations or the children and young people's committee, and speak the truth in love to a volunteer who is not considered appropriate. Friends in selecting volunteers need to bear in mind Query 18, in the first chapter of *Quaker faith & practice*: 'How can we make the meeting a community in which each person is accepted and nurtured, and strangers are welcome? Seek to know one another in the things which are eternal, bear the burden of each other's failings and pray for one another. As we enter with tender sympathy into the joys and sorrows of each other's lives, ready to give help and to receive it, our meeting can be a channel for God's love and forgiveness.'

This Query contains so much which is germane to life in modern meetings. It causes us to consider how far we can accept others and how we treat newcomers – it doesn't make any sort of stipulation about the type of stranger whom we might accept. In fact it sets us a challenge. The bearing of 'the burden of each other's failings' probes even deeper. Meetings in large cities with many visitors and enquirers may encounter all manner of people from entirely different social backgrounds or sexual orientation who may at first appear puzzling and even threatening. We are challenged to get to know them and above all to know them in 'the things which are eternal'. When we truly know someone we are surely better able to speak the truth to that person, and to listen to his or her response.

The last line of Query 18 '. . . our meeting can be a channel for God's love and forgiveness' presents us with an ideal for which we can strive.

In protecting the children and young people in our weekly meetings, we are also protecting the adults who work with the young. Other situations, which may occur outside the walls of the meeting house – for example summer schools – need supervision just as vigilant as on Sunday mornings. Experience has shown in the past, sadly, that this has not always been the case, and on occasion there have been damaging results. Certain things may be learnt from these events. In particular, anybody present becoming suspicious of the behaviour of a participant – whether adult or young person – must be prepared to speak out and help. We must be ready to overcome initial embarrassment and awkwardness. Friends sometimes fail to address such issues because they think it would not be kind. Those working professionally with children invariably warn that people in meeting who are not known to us as sex-offenders but who are behaving in an unsafe way pose a much greater threat to children in meeting than ex-offenders known to us. *Meeting Safety* gives full guidance to meetings on prevention, response and care.

In this chapter we have focused exclusively on the care of children and young people. However, we need to remember that there are adults who are vulnerable to sexual and other abuse, too. We must apply the same measures of protection, care and support to vulnerable adults.

In the words of an experienced Friend who has in the past had to mediate in some very painful situations: 'The truth must be spoken in love.' We have to strike a fair balance between recognising the humanity of the perpetrator and the need of the victim to heal. 'We mustn't be soft in the hope of the perpetrator stopping.'

Matters for Reflection

For the individual:

◆ *Am I sufficiently aware of how the signs of abuse manifest themselves in children?*

◆ *If I feel apprehension on behalf of someone, what do I say, and to whom?*

For the meeting:

◆ *How do we discern who may work with children and young people in our meeting?*

◆ *If allegations are made in a meeting how do we deal with them? Who needs to know?*

◆ *How do we care for those who may be hurt or offended when their offer to work with the young has to be refused?*

6

Lead us not into temptation but deliver us from evil

Let us suppose that in the meeting there happens to be someone who has in the past committed a Schedule 1 offence and who may have served a prison sentence for this. Schedule 1 offenders may be disqualified from working with children, and may have other conditions imposed, as part of the sentence. Were this to come to light, a survivor of abuse might well find that he or she either no longer wishes to attend meeting or at best feels very uneasy when in the presence of that person. If the offence was committed against a child, any parents in the meeting may well feel very troubled.

This is a very difficult situation and might well result in the withdrawal of one or more people from the meeting unless there is honesty on both sides – what Tim Newell writing on restorative justice calls 'transparency'.

Douglas Rennie, a social worker in childcare, says that 'we want to welcome people to meeting on the basis of their humanity, but we must protect people. We have to temper our welcome with the knowledge that they might reoffend. We greet "that of God" within them, but George Fox was also speaking about trampling down evil, not people'.[27]

A probation officer, whose clients often come into the sex offender category, warns against being 'drawn into the offender's construction of events'. This, she thinks, can easily happen with Friends because of their belief in reconciliation, in understanding all parties to a conflict, and the wish to trust. We should also bear in mind that sex offenders tend often to be better educated than many other prisoners.

So how might it be for the person released from prison? Anyone on the Sex Offenders Register is often regarded by the general public as a social pariah. During the prison sentence he or she will already have experienced what this exclusion means. Such a prisoner will have been held on a special Vulnerable Prisoners' wing, segregated from other prisoners so that he or she will not be attacked by them. He or she will have acquired the name 'nonce' or 'beast' from prisoners in other wings. Probably the person has very low self-esteem, which would have had a great bearing on the nature of the offence committed and would certainly not be improved by this exclusion.

We should not assume that all people on the Sex Offenders Register have committed the same type of offence, or are equally dangerous. For example, some convicted of indecent exposure may pose very little threat to the general public.

In the course of the prison sentence the person may have attended a Sex Offender Treatment Programme, though some refuse to participate because they are 'in denial', denying their offence or denying that they hurt anyone. On such a Programme prisoners must individually confront their offence and take ownership of it and address the behaviour which caused it.

Sex offenders, contrary to what the popular press would lead us to suppose, have a very low rate of re-offending. In a study carried out for the Home Office [28] a group of 162 serious sex offenders were followed up for four years after they had been released from prison to see how many had reoffended and in what ways. Of these, 94 were followed up for a further two years.

We are often led to believe that sex offenders – particularly ones who have been in prison for a long time – are almost inevitably going to re-offend, but that is not what the figures show. Even among those studied six years after their release, under one tenth had been re-convicted for another sexual offence.

Some of the group (82 of the 162) had been assessed by the Parole Board as being 'high risk', yet after four years only seven of those had been re convicted of a sexual offence.

The type of victim they had previously assaulted made a difference. Most noticeably, men who had abused children in their own family were very unlikely to be re-convicted – in fact none of those who had been in prison for a crime of this kind were re-convicted of a sexual offence or a serious violent offence during the period studied. Men who had raped or sexually assaulted adults had a fairly low re-conviction rate – 7.5% after six years. However, those who had abused children outside the family were much more likely to reoffend – over a quarter were reconvicted of a sexual crime within six years.

One finding that surprised the researchers is that men who denied their offence – often thought to be high risk, partly because they then don't go through a Sex Offender Treatment Programme – were unlikely to be re convicted.

We should note that re-conviction rates are not the same as re-offending rates, and that all those who were re-convicted of a sexual offence committed very serious crimes for which they received long prison sentences. We need to consider both the probability of any individual offending, and the likely damage resulting from any offence.

Sex offending is learned behaviour. Paedophiles learn how to abuse over many years and they learn how to hide their actions. Treatment has to look at the cycle of re-offending and interrupt it. Someone who has learned how to interrupt the cycle, and has support, can become a full member of society but will always need to avoid certain situations.

Some offenders' stories

O is a Friend who has served a prison sentence for a Schedule 1 offence. He is very upset by the way people condemn him, though knowing very little about him. 'We need general rules but to apply the general rules to all individuals is invidious.' Thinking back to his time in prison O says that 'amongst the people on the wing most had committed their offence for something other than the sexual – the motivation was confusion and inadequacy'.

He thinks that the Sex Offender Treatment Programme, which he underwent, was excellent because it forced him to examine his behaviour and accept responsibility for it. 'By the time we are released we are all aware of our reasons for having ended up in prison. Breaking the cycle of gratification isn't easy.'

O feels that if those who served a sentence for sexual abuse are to be integrated into meeting, total openness is necessary. Those who are responsible for him need a complete disclosure, he feels, though it is not clear whether he means the whole Quaker community or certain officers of the meeting. 'I want to move away from my offence but I must do this on an honest basis. I only entered into membership after I had undertaken the Sex Offender Treatment Programme. I was conscious that people needed to know what I had done and what I had undergone in order that they could decide whether or not to accept me.'

When O was taken into prison the Quaker Prison Minister who saw him said, 'You've got yourself into a nice mess here.' He was very struck by the fact that the QPM wasn't judgmental but placed the responsibility on O himself. This made him feel that he must strive to become worthy of Friends.

Often offenders and ex-prisoners are unwilling to meet those against whom they have offended, but in O's case the relatives of the person concerned have refused to meet him. 'I have never been able to hear the anger and hurt of the parents of my victim.'

Life for O as a member of his meeting is fretted with problems. These of course continue in the outer world too. 'I can't ever volunteer for things. The label has been stuck on my forehead. I've got my yellow star. Society wants its scapegoats.'

O's actions, he feels, are invariably open to misinterpretation. One incident has made a deep impression on him. Someone in his meeting who knows of his past offending had a baby, and one Sunday when the baby was three weeks old, the mother asked O to hold the child for a few minutes whilst she was attending to something. O felt very moved to be holding this tiny baby. It was only later that he heard of the rumblings of dismay from others who had expressed horror that O, a former sex offender, should have been allowed to hold the child. What has made it worse, O feels, is that nobody ever approached him directly about their views.

O returns often to the need for honesty in relationships: 'Absolute honesty is the base of everything.' He stresses that support groups need to have foreknowledge of the offender and the risk assessment. Before leaving prison they are assessed as to the risk of their re-offending. This is obviously important knowledge for support groups to have.

Of Friends generally O thinks they show 'a reluctance to indulge in any emotion other than enthusiasm – negative emotions need to be expiated'. He feels that his meeting doesn't know how to handle his negative emotions. 'When I'm down, I stop talking.' The value of a support group is that it enables people to clarify the situation and there can be a dialogue.

*

Another man who served a prison sentence for sexual abuse, P, thinks that Friends are being drawn into the present national mood of hysteria. 'They are becoming legalistic and prescriptive. *Safeguarding our Children from Harm* is prescriptive. There ought to be more plain speaking and room for people to behave in a common sense way. "The letter killeth but the Spirit giveth life".' [29]

Something of which P does approve is the recently set up Circles of Support and Accountability system, in which a carefully selected and prepared group offers both care and challenge, on a long-term basis, to help a sex-offender be safe enough to become a part of normal society again. These Circles are described in full in chapter 7, page 43.

How does a meeting understand all the strands in a complex story? P's is complicated by another element, which the telling of it reveals.

'Twenty-five years ago, at the age of 36, I was in serious trouble with the law: I was sexually involved with [young] teenage boys, at a time when the age of consent for homosexual acts between men was 21. The four brothers concerned came from a deprived family, one of several I was working with as a student, and whose history led to social ostracism at the time I first knew them . . . The oldest, Q, was eight when I first knew him, a child of low intelligence in academic terms, but of great character, as well as striking physical beauty . . . Knowing Q was the most formative influence on me as a young adult, and helped me combat the inner despair that dogged me all through that time . . . Their mother approved of the relationship I had with her sons; the father was not so sure.

'I am quite clear about the influences in my early life that led to an emotional preference for boys and young men; it goes back as far as I can remember. While I never regretted my attachment to Q, since it benefited both of us, I was uneasy that it seemed to dominate everything in my life. I sought professional help, but was dismissed with scorn – people just did not take me seriously.

'. . . We became sexual partners. I was 30, and he was 16. While not fixated on his own sex, as I was, Q could accept the same-sex relationship as he understood the strength of my feelings for him, and we did share everything else as well . . . I was however full of guilt, as I well knew I was breaking the law . . .'

Ultimately P became involved with all three of Q's younger brothers and was visited by the police. His parents' response was to want to keep the matter hidden, but P insisted on writing to all his friends and informing them. His parents were told by one Friend that sorrows as well as joys should be shared by the whole meeting. P's father was 'nonplussed by the whole subject of homosexuality, though in practical terms he knew what to do to support me'.

During the four stressful months that he was on bail P lived at the homes of two Quaker families. What upset him considerably was that Q and one of the other boys were charged as well, on the grounds that they were willing accomplices. Although the cases of the two young men never came to court, they nevertheless spent time in police custody. Friends 'turned out in force to support' P at his trial in the Crown Court, where he was sentenced to four years imprisonment. 'I was clearly a real subversive, a serious threat to society . . . This was a crushing sentence for a person who had never even had a parking ticket.'

After serving his sentence P reappeared at his own meeting. 'I believe some people did not even know I had been away. One Friend, who was a retired policeman, took me aside for a fatherly word.'

Following his imprisonment P found it well nigh impossible to get work. Finally at a Job Centre career guidance interview the interviewer told him:

'You have a double disadvantage – you're gay, and you have a criminal record. I'm not prejudiced, in fact I'm gay myself. My advice is, stop wasting time looking for work, and find something else to do with the rest of your life.' Like O, P has found his greatest difficulty when he has wanted to play a caring role as people distrust him because of his criminal record. However he has managed to surmount this problem.

'The real breakthrough came when I got involved in voluntary work, which proved more fulfilling than anything people were prepared to pay me to do, and now takes three forms. My commitment to the Society of Friends takes as much time as I am prepared to give it. I have served on a variety of Quaker committees . . . I joined Quakers in Criminal Justice as soon as it was set up . . .'

P implies that the meeting may have more of a problem with his homosexuality than with his offences against the young. He knows that he is not allowed to share any activities for children in the meeting. He says however that 'if my local meeting started telling me which occasions I could and could not attend, I would leave the Society. I can talk to several individual Friends in confidence, but for the meeting as a whole to discuss homosexual issues would be unthinkable. As it is, our treasurer threatened to resign if a Quaker Lesbian and Gay Fellowship meeting went ahead in the building. Whatever did the Friend think was going to happen?'

P's story highlights a number of issues: being a homosexual does not mean that one is a paedophile. Same sex relationships like heterosexual ones may be monogamous – and even when they are not monogamous, they are not necessarily predatory. In some cases a person may be homosexual and a paedophile, just as one may be heterosexual and a paedophile. It is also clear from P's story that his life has been clouded and that he has suffered a great deal through feelings of isolation and alienation because of his offences, but that he has nevertheless managed to come to terms with his situation and has done much valuable work for Friends and for society in general.

*

R's situation, as he describes it below, has some similarities with P's but in other ways it is completely dissimilar. At the moment serving a sentence and attending Quaker meeting in prison R has, like P, always known that he was gay and in his case, has invariably been attracted to boys around the age of nine or ten. After seeing an advert on the internet from a man living fairly near his home, someone with a nine year old son, he became involved with the boy's father and eventually moved in with him. A year or so later R began sexually offending against his partner's son.

'I convinced myself that my step-son would be willing and that it was what he wanted as much as I. The offending continued for over a year until my arrest.' R has completed both the Core and the Booster programmes of the Sex Offender Treatment Programme and he says of these 'They have been a great help to me in coming to terms with what I've done, and most importantly to me, in accepting the *wrongness* of my thoughts and actions as opposed to the mere illegality. Leading up to my offending and during my offending I used many excuses to give myself permission to offend: he's old enough, he's physically mature.

Nobody will get hurt, he wants it as much as I do, we love each other . . . the list is endless.

'I believe my biggest excuse was the distorted attitude that there was nothing wrong with having sex with a child provided that the child was willing. This attitude stayed with me until part way through the Core SOTP. Through another inmate's account of his offence, I realised that consent is only valid if it is informed and freely given. I recognise now that a child does not have the emotional maturity to give free and informed consent. Although I didn't use physical force, the emotional pressure on my step-son was so strong, he really had no option but to yield to my wishes.

'Obviously I am in a position to speak with many other sexual offenders and my impression is that my feelings are mirrored in many cases. We all manage to convince ourselves that what we're doing isn't wrong. It is also my opinion that most people leave this prison with an appreciation of the effect their offending has had on others and a sincere desire not to re-offend. Those who leave with a good strong support network have the best chance of success. This is why I consider Circles of Support and Accountability an excellent idea. The more support an ex-offender is given, the less likely he or she is to re-offend, which must be advantageous to both the ex-offender and society. There is nothing I can do for my ex-partner and his son, but if I can do anything to assist other potential victims of sexual offending, I shall do my best.'

*

S has attended Friends' meetings and is currently serving a second prison sentence for a sex offence: 'I detest what I did, I had no excuses, although I realise God will forgive me, I haven't forgiven myself. I don't know if I ever will. Anyway, I had the strange experience of my victim writing to me, saying she had forgiven me through her faith in God.'

S had committed the same type of offence, again, to the one for which he had been convicted about ten years before, when he sexually assaulted his wife after drugging her. 'I was arrested and sent to jail. In prison I was told I should go to Grendon Under-wood, the therapeutic prison, to address my perversion. Then I was told, "Shut up, get on with your sentence". So I "switched off" to my perversion and concentrated on doing Open University courses. I ran away in my mind from my crime.'

Whilst he was in prison the first time he managed to apply for and get a post at a university, one which also necessitated S looking after student accommodation. 'Back then I wasn't on licence because there was no Sex Offenders Register, so I was successfully merged back into society. The problem was, though, that I had not rid myself of my sexual perversion. So this resulted in my re-offending against my partner – the same thing – hence my arrest in 2000.

'Before I was sent to prison in 1985 I was not in regular attend-ance at meeting. At that time I deluded myself that I didn't have a problem. Of course I had. This time, since being in prison again, I have done the Sex Offender Treatment Core Programme. And I am planning to apply to Dovegate and Grendon Underwood to rid myself of my offending behaviour.

'On release? Well, personally, what I seek is a place where I can play an active part back in the community. I will be about sixty then, so I have the idea that after spending time in a hostel, I might find a place with the Society of Friends – I don't want to be in hiding, I want to help others. I have heard of the Circles of Support and Accountability in the South of England. So my case is probably different from those of many offenders as my behaviour is very specific.'

S warns: 'Some prisoners are very manipulative, devious and dangerous and pose a real threat to Friends, who try to help them. Many prisoners are not very bright; some are socially inadequate; some have learning difficulties. So Friends need a very good risk assessment of any offender. Any Friends' support team needs to be well trained and not naïve to risks. However, I am totally convinced that Friends can play a major role in the successful re-settlement of sex offenders.'

*

The stories and musings give us an insight into the wide range of criminal behaviour, which is subsumed under the general heading 'sex offence'. Indeed sex offenders are not a particular type of person, they are ordinary individuals. This should perhaps lead us to the realisation that no single answer will ever be adequate for dealing with the problem which may arise of how to integrate people who have served a prison sentence for sexual abuse into the life of meetings.

Matters for Reflection

+ *In what ways can we support an ex-offender in our meeting?*
+ *How can we reach a balance between trust and watchfulness?*
+ *What do we understand by 'that of God' in an abuser? How might we seek it?*

7
Help in Responding

In the present climate of fear and hysteria, and with Britain's prisons at bursting point and the media feeding the public's demand for more draconian measures to be taken against sex offenders, it has become apparent that for humanity's sake something must be done. We already impose longer prison sentences than most other countries in the Western world.

John Lampen thinks that from childhood we have been educated to believe 'that badness is only kept in check by harshness, not by understanding and love. The calls in society for executions, floggings and imprisonment for life stem from this illusion that it is only violent controls which prevent chaos breaking out all around us – and not only round us but inside us too.'[30]

Are we in this country going to continue, growing ever more punitive, and shall we lock away abusers until they die in prison? And if not, then what is the alternative?

It is already, and always has been, very difficult for ex-prisoners who have committed offences against property to be accepted by a world outside the sub-culture in which many of them would normally live, and which is often largely responsible for their offending in the first place. Sex offenders have this difficulty compounded because they bear the brand of the untouchable, the unsavoury. Shunning people does not help them nor the society at large. In fact it intensifies the ex-offenders' feeling of alienation and returns them to an obsessive shadow world of secrecy, where further offences may likely be committed.

There is another possibility, in the example set by Circles of Support and Accountability, a Canadian idea that Quakers in this country have piloted and are promoting.

Circles of support and accountability

A few years ago a Canadian Friends Service Committee newsletter mentioned a project being piloted by the Mennonite Church. Friends in this country thought that a similar project might be transferable to the United Kingdom. Subsequently an approach was made to the Dangerous Offenders Unit at the Home Office. As a result of this, in June 2000 a workshop was hosted jointly by Quaker Social Responsibility & Education and the Dangerous Offenders Unit – the purpose being to look into how the Correctional Service of Canada uses Circles of Support and Accountability, and to consider the establishing of a working group to oversee pilot projects in England. At this workshop were five Canadians who explained how the scheme was being conducted in Canada.

In the Mennonite manual *Community Reintegration Project: circles of support and accountability*,[31] guiding principles are:

- We believe in a loving and reconciling God who calls us to be agents of healing work in the world.
- We recognise the humanity of both the victim and the offender.
- We acknowledge the ongoing pain and the need for healing victims of sexual abuse.
- We affirm that only love has the potential to heal the wounds of the victim, the offender and the community. This love is lived out in the context of meaningful and accountable relationships where support and care takes a human face.
- We welcome the offender into the community and account-

ability. Where this does not exist for them, we seek to 'recreate community' with them in responsible, safe, healthy, and life-giving ways.

- We seek to prevent further victimisation both through reducing recidivism by offenders and increasing public awareness in the wider community. It is through education about the roots of violence and abuse that our communities become safer.
- We accept God's call to radical hospitality, sharing our lives with one another in community and taking on risks in the service of love.

The Mennonite aims expressed here are very much in line with Friends' thinking, as they are mindful of the needs of both the victim and the offender and are working to establish a safer and more just society.

The decision was taken at this workshop to consider the best ways of helping a similar scheme to the Canadian one to be run in this country.

Since that time some experimental Circles of Support and Accountability have indeed been established in the United Kingdom. One of these pilot programmes is being run by Quaker Peace & Social Witness.

These Circles comprise four to six volunteers drawn from the local community, each with a high risk sex offender who is the 'core member'. The Circle is established to work with a particular offender and can call on the support and advice of a Circles staff member and the local multi-agency team, including the Probation Service.

At the outset a contract is drawn up between the core member and the other members: the core member must state that there will be no more victims of abuse at his hands. The volunteers are trained and supported in their work, which they will continue initially for a year. At first the whole group will meet weekly and perhaps organise a rota for contacting the core member more frequently. The idea is to make regular contact with the core member, meeting for a chat or a visit to a local café, informal outings to give the person a feeling of being able to do ordinary activities along with friends. Many sexual offenders have been rejected by their families because of the abuse they committed and are completely alone, except perhaps for others with whom they might have met up in prison. Isolation can only deepen people's self-destructive tendencies.

The support of the Circle thus has benefits to the community at large: it helps prevent the creating of new victims, and it may help offenders to lead useful lives and integrate them into the rest of society. Circles of Support and Accountability have the potential to dissipate the present tendency to demonise the sexual offender and rob him or her of their humanity.

At the very heart of Circles of Support and Accountability is the idea of restorative justice, which recognises the needs of both the victim and the abuser. Some people may at first voice scepticism regarding the viability of such a system because they feel that too much emphasis is invariably placed on offender rehabilitation. Their doubts might be justified if this were only about 'support', but it is also about 'accountability'.

The offender is being held accountable for his or her actions and the circle assists in this by being there and offering friendship and a framework within which the offender can live. The circle works *with* the core member to build up new ways of life which avoid temptations and trigger points. Where there is trust, there can be miracles, but we need to be able to believe in the essential humanity of one another. Circles Support are not 'soft' on the person who has abused; they are being realistic about human frailty but are also acknowledging that behaviour can change; that old habits can fall away, given the right environment.

In a venture such as this there will of course be risks, particularly were a much-publicised case to go badly wrong – but then an element of risk is almost inevitable in anything which is groundbreaking and innovative. Circles are alert to signs of danger, and the core member knows they may have to take action to prevent abuse by reporting him to the police. As we noted

45

above, the founding contract of each Circle is 'no more victims at my hands'.

Commitment to a Circle is demanding work, for the volunteers as for the core member.

The James Nayler Foundation

Someone whose work could complement Circles of Support and Accountability is the psychiatrist Bob Johnson, who has set up the James Nayler Foundation for working with those people labelled 'personality disordered' and 'incurable'. He has discovered through his work in high security prisons that behind the most violently abusive acts lie childhood experiences of gross abuse; he believes that through humane treatment the injuries in people resulting from such histories may be healed, so that the offenders cease to offend.

The Foundation takes its name from James Nayler, an early Quaker, who declared as he lay dying from a severe beating, in 1660: 'There is a spirit which I feel that delights to do no evil, nor to revenge any wrong . . . Its hope is to outlive all wrath and contention, and to weary out all exaltation and cruelty. It takes its kingdom with entreaty and not with contention . . .' This quotation sums up the aspirations of the Foundation.

Quaker Prison Ministers

Another group of people who are working with sex offenders are of course Quaker Prison Ministers, who are part of a prison chaplaincy team. Because of their contact with offenders whilst they are in prison they may learn to see them as real people and not stereotypes, though sometimes to reach this position isn't easy. One Quaker Prison Minister facilitating an 'Alternatives to Violence' weekend for the first time on a vulnerable prisoners unit where most of the prisoners were sex offenders felt very uneasy at the thought of how things might go wrong.

'I thought of the cramped kitchen where we would be making coffees and teas and I had to put a brake on my imaginings. We would be spending the next eighteen or so hours with a group of twelve or so inmates whom we didn't know but who all came under the general heading of "sex offender". In this unit we would be totally alone – well of course we had a radio – but a call for help from us would indicate that we had failed.

'So there we were in the chapel on the first morning. A huge chap shambled in. His face was craggy with the life he had lived. "Well," he said, the moment he came into the room, "I'm doing ten years for rape and violence." "Actually we didn't want to know about that," I said, though I went cold and felt as though I had received ice cold water dashed in my face.

'By the end of the weekend that man had become a real person for us and not a monster. He was a simple soul, from a very poor and violent background, struggling with basic literacy but managing to achieve goals. He had a sense of humour and took part in all our activities in a thoughtful way.

'We have since run other workshops on this unit and I have completely lost my feelings of apprehension about those taking part.'

Speaking personally, I know that a prison minister might, however, sometimes inadvertently complicate matters for a meeting when it is deciding how to react to the presence of a former sex offender in its midst. Because of working in prison and having grown accustomed to dealing with people who may have committed grievous offences, the prison minister could very well adopt a more relaxed approach to the matter than the meeting in general. Other members of the meeting may find the views of some prison ministers incomprehensible and even frightening. And as we shall see in the next chapter (page 57), Quaker prison ministers and their local meetings need to discern the right way to support a prisoner who is drawn to membership.

Matters for Reflection

- *How do I react to these new developments in the treatment of sex abusers?*

- *In what ways, if any, might I be able to offer service in such projects?*

- *Am I keeping abreast of new ideas for creating a safer community?*

- *What can our meeting learn from the Project, even if we cannot set up a full-scale Circle ourselves?*

8
The Experience of
Some Meetings

Anumber of Quaker meetings in England, Scotland and Wales have had to consider the practical implications of receiving into their midst someone who was convicted of a sex offence. In cases where the meeting had not thought through the possibility of having a sex offender worshipping with them, there seems to have been a certain amount of confusion.

*

Friends in Meeting I, for example, were totally unprepared when an approach was made by the police enquiring as to whether an ex-offender might attend. A group of four met with the police who explained the nature of the offender's licence, which precluded him from contact with children. A special preparative meeting (a business meeting of the local Quaker group) was convened where the matter was discussed and everyone was made aware of the situation.

The local meeting decided that although they did not at the time have any children attending regularly, they did not feel that it would be right for the ex-offender to take part in the meeting for worship. They did however ask the elders and overseers of the wider monthly or area meeting to think how Meeting I might support this person The over-riding view seemed to be that the protection of children and vulnerable people in the meeting must be Friends' chief concern. Members said that they did not have the resources anyway to form some kind of circle which could support and hold the ex-prisoner accountable.

A further reason, which some local Quakers voiced as to why the ex-offender should not be admitted, was the smallness of meeting I, where there tends to be far greater contact between people and an atmosphere of greater intimacy arises. As Friends often have group activities this could add a further strain to the matter of having someone had committed sexual abuse amongst them.

One member of this small Quaker community, U, who takes a different view of how Meeting I ought to have responded to this situation, says that he has been very surprised how strong the reaction has been from people known to him for years. He had expected them to react differently and U was taken aback by how vocal they were in their response. He thinks that their opinion was also swayed by the letter of a survivor of abuse which appeared in *Quaker News* under the title, 'Caring for sex offenders – okay, but what about the victims?' 'We were saying we were protecting the children, but we weren't.'

For this Friend the very essence of Quakerism is that we should be welcoming everyone to meeting and the sudden discovery that so many think otherwise has been very painful for him. On the positive side U says, 'It jolts you up and makes you spiritually aware. It has also brought a group of people together. I am surprised who has come forward.' He thinks that all the members of the meeting have learnt a great deal about one another because of this situation, though some feel that they have failed.

Looking back over what has happened, U thinks that part of the problem was caused also by the released prisoner being totally unknown. No-one local had in fact met him, with the exception of the handful of people who had visited him in prison and have now made contact with him on his release.

*

Meeting II has found itself having to face the fact that one of its members, V, had committed a sexual offence for which he was sent to prison. The meeting approached the situation in this way.

Once Meeting II learned the facts of V's offending, several Friends wrote to or visited him regularly in prison whilst he was awaiting trial. He appreciated this very much, because he felt that he had not been totally abandoned. Many thought that it was essential to remain non-judgmental and felt challenged by this principle – to hold him as a person, whilst knowing his behaviour had led to his arrest.

Other questions of principle can emerge. How should we hold or share knowledge?

What made the situation more difficult in this case was the fact that V had asked that the news of his abuse should be limited to a small section of the Quaker meeting, who were meant to keep the case secret. This secrecy caused some Friends to feel hurt and excluded whilst others passed on rumours.

Members of Meeting II consider that if an offender asks for total confidentiality he or she is forcing the meeting into a very difficult position. It places an almost unacceptable obligation on those individuals, who are part of the meeting community. Also sadly this became counter productive because some Friends read of the offence in the local paper anyway. The reason why V had asked for confidentiality was because he had not told his parents. In the event, after the passage of several weeks visiting Friends persuaded him to do so. This openness enabled a small number of Friends to act as a support team for his parents.

A visit, which did not prove successful, was made by several from the meeting who visited him as a 'prison experience' – they were not close to him at all – and he told the group who did visit regularly that he had found the newcomers very voyeuristic.

Looking back over this experience, Quakers in Meeting II think that some things ought to have been handled differently. In the event of such a situation arising again, they would bring together an emergency meeting of overseers and elders to decide on a response to the matter, to look at support strategies for the individual and his/her family, and to consider what to do about managing community issues in the meeting and members' reactions.

After serving his sentence V is now living elsewhere, but some of the members of his original meeting have kept in touch with him.

＊

Those in Meeting III have worked out their own way of coping with the presence of someone on the Sex Offenders Register. They hold two regular meetings anyway: he attends the mid-week meeting, not the Sunday worship.

Parents at the smaller Meeting IV elsewhere in the same city had said that they couldn't have the sex offender attending there. Parents of the under-fives didn't see the presence of an ex-offender as a big issue, because children of this age group are under close supervision the whole time. With older children the situation is more difficult, and the openness of the meeting house becomes a problem. Even so, two of the parents in Meeting IV were of the view that it would not be of significant concern, because wherever you go, you may unknowingly come upon sex abusers. They considered it their own responsibility to watch out for their children. Their attitude was that you can protect children from a known person.

At Meeting III's mid-week gathering, which has accepted the former offender, the issue of confidentiality has arisen: the children's committee has not been told of the man's identity, as it was felt that he has the right to have this knowledge withheld – and he is not attending on Sundays when the children are present. However, various other groups of adults may be using the building. He has been given an agreement, which he has signed and entered into. Children in Meeting III are mostly of creche age; parents have accepted the arrangements and nobody has withdrawn children from the meeting. New parents will not be informed about the matter. However everyone has been shown the video *Facing the Unthinkable*, which shows the dangers for churches as they are an open door for sex offenders.

Meeting III asked the former prisoner and representatives of the meeting to sign an agreement, which focused just on the mid-week meeting for worship. The offender agreed when he would be in the building and how he would behave. The members of the mid-week meeting agreed to oversee him and specified which information would be kept confidential. The agreement was to be reviewed regularly and revised as necessary.

*

In another city, an abuse survivors' organisation became very upset that an ex-offender could enter a Quaker meeting and accused the Quakers of putting children at risk. After they learned of the safety measures which were in place they were reassured.

*

At Meeting V the difficulties arose because not all parents of young children knew that an ex-offender had begun to attend meeting. The news reached some of them through whispers, and nobody seemed prepared to speak openly of the matter. This led to one parent on the children's committee leaving the meeting. She felt angry that those responsible had the power to withhold information and she felt they were patronising and misguided. 'I feel all sexual offenders are a risk.' She is of the view that new parents should be told if someone who served a sentence for a sex offence is attending the meeting.

Another member of the children's committee, W, who also left Meeting V over the same matter, felt that 'it was mainly to do with lack of communication, and confusion. We said we would adopt *Safeguarding Children from Harm*, the handbook now superseded by *Meeting Safety*, as a safety policy. At a national meeting the matter of a sex offender in meeting came up and we were told that all those on the children's committee should be told about such an offender. We took this information back to our meeting. The key issue was the right to know – not necessarily the need to know the identity of the person – it all crystallised round this issue. We contacted overseers about the matter and all they said was "I don't know what your problem is". The upshot of all this was that the meeting decided that it was wrong to inform the parents of children in the meeting but they might be told in discretion.'

W was able to speak with the former prisoner directly at a 'creative listening' group, where he was able to talk about his offence. 'The secretiveness did not come from him.' What was not really taken into account was the fact that in this particular meeting there are quite a lot of known survivors of abuse. The ex-offender's support group made W feel 'you're only getting hysterical about this because you're a victim.' 'The support group,' she felt, 'were projecting their own fears into the situation.'

Looking back over the whole situation, W says, 'we felt there was a way forward – the best of all possible worlds – raising the matter in meeting was beneficial. Raising consciousness of the issues was of benefit for all concerned and important for people's safety. It was important for the ex-offender too to feel accepted. There was a win-win possibility in this situation, but we need a lot of time and energy for this.'

Unfortunately this situation has caused hurts which have been difficult to heal, and X, another of the Friends concerned in raising the matter says 'I think that this whole issue of admitting ex-offenders to meeting is going to be a minefield in an organisation that is historically and presently passionate about rehabilitation. In fact the deep sympathy that many Friends expressed towards the offender seemed to make it hard for them to empathise with potential or actual victims.' X feels that although it is wonderful that a meeting should be supportive of someone who is effectively an outsider to the rest of society, she has never heard any expression of concern for the man's victim. 'Members and attenders who bring "difficult" issues into the light need support.' X and another former member of the meeting's children's committee were made to feel 'victims' in view of all that happened. She thinks group dynamics played a large part in causing the upheaval.

Something can surely be learnt from the experience of Meeting V: we must beware of allowing our liberal sympathies to push us in a direction which may cause distress to other vulnerable people on the way.

This story highlights yet again the need for communication between people in meeting, and above all transparency and honesty. Unless we discuss matters openly and try to empathise with others, we cannot hope for a solution to difficulties, which will meet the needs of the Quaker community.

✳

Another Quaker, Y, has encountered the situation where a well-respected Friend has been given a prison sentence for sexual abuse. Y feels very strongly that this person should not be rejected by Meeting VI on his release from prison.

Meeting VI has held many meetings for clearness regarding the matter and all are agreed that this is a challenge which they must meet. 'It is an issue of how we manage our meetings and ourselves. It could be used in a productive way to strengthen our faith. When people accuse Quakerism of being woolly, this is not the case. Whether he is remorseful or not is irrelevant. Meeting should encourage the best to come out. If people have an insecure faith, they will find this difficult to accept.'

Y meets the problem head on. 'Some people think Friends are a nice safe club. People want to be comfortable when they come to meeting. Meeting is "for our comfort and our discomfort"[32] – for the comfort of sex offenders and the discomfort of others. It is no good extolling the Circles of Support and Accountability if we aren't prepared to support them in meeting. We're distancing ourselves from the real problems – this strikes at the fundamental core of what it means to be a Quaker meeting.' Some people, she thinks, prefer to have the good works 'done for them from a distance'.

These may sound like uncompromising words, yet they are well within the Quaker tradition. Quakers are not in the main a cosy group. 'Comfort' to seventeenth century Quakers meant 'fortifying together', as well as 'reassuring'. Our peace testimony may sometimes be misinterpreted as promising easy peace.

*

A very experienced mediator and Quaker, Z, visited Meeting VII which has been split down the middle by people being unable to agree on how they should approach the matter of an ex-offender being admitted to their community. Those with small children felt that they could not countenance it. Others took a more relaxed view. Elsewhere, in Meeting VIII, Quakers decided to admit to meeting for worship someone who had been imprisoned for abuse but would not allow him to take part in any social group.

These arrangements had all been made without speaking with the ex-offenders concerned. Z feels that in cases of this nature it is always better to hold a round-table meeting where people concerned about their children may put these worries to the ex-offender. In holding such a meeting it is a good idea to have a mediator present, someone who can help form a restorative group.

People, says Z, tend to rush to conclusions without really having any accurate information about the person who has served a sentence for sex abuse. They assume that the person will be a danger. If things are brought out into the open and talked about people will feel less fearful. Z is of the opinion that with over 70,000 registered sex offenders out in the community it is far better to accept someone who is willing to face up to his or her personal history rather than someone totally unknown. We must also constantly remind ourselves that most sex abuse occurs in the family or with family friends.

Looking at the panic which seems apparent in meetings when the question of admitting an ex-offender is mentioned, Z says there is a tendency for Quakers to think of sex as being 'dangerous and uncontrollable'. 'If it is for that person, what are you thinking about yourself? Because sex is hidden we find it difficult to cope with.'

Whilst cautioning against behaving in a condemnatory way towards all former sex-offenders, Z draws on her experience of mediation to say that anyone with this type of background should be challenged as to his or her behaviour. 'Someone who has abused trust cannot expect to deserve trust. Such people must prove over time that they are trustworthy.'

Formal membership

A situation has arisen in a number of meetings where someone whose offences have been against children has been accepted into membership of a monthly (regional) meeting of the Society of Friends whilst in prison. Upon his release he has then wanted to worship in one of the local meetings of the region but has found this difficult. In some cases former abusers have been able to meet only with a small group of Friends on an irregular basis. What is particularly painful here is that after being accepted into formal membership such a person would naturally assume that he would be welcomed into the meeting.

It is perhaps very unwise to accept into membership serving prisoners (whatever their offence) who have never attended a meeting for worship in the larger community outside prison. Prison meetings for worship cannot possibly replicate the atmosphere of community meetings, because the circumstances in prison are so different – and after all the meeting for worship is both the foundation and an expression of the spiritual life of a community. The Quaker Prison Ministers' handbook does in fact caution against the acceptance of serving prisoners into membership. Prisoners should perhaps be made aware that many people attend meeting in the community for a considerable number of years before seeking membership – and some in fact prefer to continue as life-long attenders. Formal membership is not a prerequisite for worshipping with Quakers or becoming a part of the community. If this is made clear to prisoners it can prevent a later feeling of rejection and hurt.

Thinking it through

It is clear that varying approaches will evolve over time: we need to learn from each other's experience. If an increasing number of ex-offenders wish to worship with Friends, the meetings will be more able to take on the challenge.

Some Friends suggest that, in order to prevent the situation arising where people act instinctively and do not really examine why they have reached their views, it would be helpful if the members, before discussing the idea of receiving an ex-offender into meeting for worship, could talk first with the key probation people in the area. This could be done before the released prisoner appeared. By doing this the risks and benefits can be weighed up and the meeting can find out what support it may be offered – support differs from area to area. The statutory obligations are the same but the way these are carried out may differ.

This mode of approach can set realistic targets and people will then see whether they can cope. However, it does depend on ample notice being given of an ex-offender wishing to get involved in a specific Quaker community.

There are two parties to any agreement. If sex offenders wish to come to a Quaker meeting for worship or other activities, they should accept the constraints. We have to keep reminding ourselves too of the distinction between the crime and the person. At the same time there have to be limits beyond which we cannot go.

The scenario could arise where an ex-offender is attending a meeting where someone is present who had been abused. We may not actually know that anyone present is a survivor, but statistics suggest that there will be survivors among the worshippers at most Quaker meetings. The former abuser may not have attacked a particular survivor, but nonetheless she may feel vulnerable and be distressed.

Perhaps the sex-offender might attend worship every second

week. Survivors could quietly attend the alternate weeks. In these kinds of situation we need to employ an imaginative approach, which will take account of the feelings of all concerned as far as possible. Each case may require a different solution.

In several meetings the situation has arisen where it has come to Friends' notice that a member or regular attender has in the past committed a Schedule 1 sexual offence, for which he has only now received a prison sentence. The shock to Friends of having to recognise that someone they have known for years has done such a thing has in some cases caused a great deal of consternation. First, there has been rage that a person whom they trusted with their children had in fact at one time committed an act of this nature. Suddenly what they have always believed to be a safe environment no longer is so. Then there is confusion that this person has had areas in his life which have remained totally hidden from his fellow Quakers – and this over many years.

This type of news can reach individuals, perhaps the clerk, overseers or other officers of the meeting, as an allegation. Naturally we would want to assume that some mistake has been made, that such information cannot possibly be true, and of course false allegations may arise. We are left with the fear of making a dreadful mistake, but a decision must be reached on how to ascertain facts. We can, of course, take refuge in Quaker silence – but what if the allegation is founded on the truth? If the person concerned has been abusing children for many years, by remaining silent we may be conniving at abuse. This is a very difficult decision to have to make, and rendered harder if we have known the person for a long time and been a personal friend.

If, let us say, only one or two know of this matter and they learn that the allegation is true, do they inform the entire meeting of it? Being alone in possession of this knowledge can be very isolating. Whom should they tell? Does the whole meeting need to know? Suppose the information spread beyond the meeting, to the neighbourhood, perhaps to the press? What about the accused? If responsible members such as the clerk and overseers are going to act with transparency perhaps they ought to speak with him at the outset. This leads us back to the *Advice* to 'seek to know one another in the things which are eternal'.[33] If we really do communicate with others in the Quaker community on a level beyond surface talk it might be possible to speak the truth and to learn the truth even in something as painful and traumatic as this. We might also be enabled to look beyond the crime to the person because it is possible to hate one whilst feeling affection for the other.

In a situation where the whole meeting apart from, say, the clerk and overseers remain in the dark about what has happened and do not learn the truth until after the offender has been sentenced, parents could feel outraged, children made anxious and survivors of past traumatic incidents might feel increasingly insecure. For this reason in similar situations it would seem far better to share the information carefully with such people and take steps to consult someone in the Local Authority Child Protection area.

It is possible though, that Friends might feel reluctant to involve officialdom. Perhaps they do not know who to contact. Of course within the monthly meeting there may already be the resource people to help and advise on the way forward. There are voluntary organisations that can provide help (see the Appendix 4 on page 94).

When an offender is known to the meeting, another tricky area will be how the meeting copes with his release at the end of his sentence. In advance the meeting's officers along with the parents of the meeting's children and the children's committee will need to draw up a contract for the ex-offender to sign so that he can know the framework within which he will remain. A Circle of Support and Accountability, which looks to the wider community and draws on multi-agency support, may not be practical or appropriate, but we can learn from the principle of making a very clear and detailed agreement about safe behaviour.

For all parties in this situation there will no doubt be feelings of embarrassment and awkwardness and, at times, disbelief until everyone grows used to the new system. The former prisoner may feel mortification, acute shame and remorse, though it is possible that members of the meeting will consider that he does not show sufficient remorse – it does after all take a long time for anger and disbelief to subside. The feelings of betrayal experienced by parents of small children, if they were never truly taken into account in the first place, are bound to linger on. Worst though perhaps will be the inevitable distaste with which they may be gripped when they must once more meet someone who has committed sexual abuse. They will wonder too: when did the offences start? How many unknown children have been hurt by this person? Has the abuse ceased? These worries will be more acute if the ex-offender is a young person, and potentially at the start of an offending career. There will most certainly be a gulf separating such a former prisoner from the rest of the meeting.

Perhaps we should remember the words of Elizabeth Fry, the prison reformer, where she was writing of her work: 'Much depends on the spirit in which the visitor enters upon her work. It must be in the spirit, not of judgement, but of mercy. She must not say in her heart *I am more holy than thou* but must rather keep in perpetual remembrance that 'all have sinned and come short of the Glory of God.'[34] An awareness of our own flaws, whatever they are, can help us try to understand – though not to excuse – the offender.

Elizabeth Fry was able, because of her absolute belief in the Divine in all people, to undertake work in prison, which was in its day revolutionary. For us today the challenge is a different one. Oh yes, we are trying to follow in her footsteps with work in prison, but what are we doing when the prisoner is released into the community. Are we going to say 'so far and no further'? This is not to diminish the difficulty of the task. Very often it is hard to feel sympathy for people who have committed sexual abuse. Elizabeth Fry's task of entering the prisons of her time, where the conditions would have been appalling, will not have been easy either. She worked amongst the verminous and the uneducated, the violent and the desperate, probably people with whom she would have had very little in common, but she was able to see beyond their crimes and their outward condition to their essential human core.

One meeting's example

Throughout the country meetings have been deliberating on how to work out *a modus vivendi* with regard to the issue of accepting Schedule 1 sex offenders into meeting. The elders of Meeting IX drew up clear guidance which they felt might be of help to others in their monthly or area meeting.

> The experience of other meetings, and our own, seemed to show that things had become most difficult when the meeting had not prepared itself in any way for the possibility that someone on the Sex Offenders Register might wish to come to meeting for worship. The difficulties seemed to arise when Friends were trying to decide how to respond at the same time as the situation was unfolding.
>
> A Standing Committee should be appointed forthwith, consisting of Warden and Clerk (these two being the most likely Friends to be approached by Probation or other outside agencies) together with an Elder, an Overseer and a member of the Children's Committee. This Committee to be encouraged to co-opt another Friend with specialist experience which might apply to any particular case. In the event of a request, or information being received, the Committee would be convened quickly . . .
>
> The Committee would be responsible for reaching an agreement with the ex-offender about any special conditions required for his or her attendance at Meeting for Worship (e.g. having a group of two or three Friends appointed to look after him/her). It was envisaged that one or two members of the Committee would make contact with the ex-offender, rather than the whole group . . .

The purpose of the exercise would thus not be to decide *whether* a person may attend meeting for worship, but whether the person can agree to the safeguards (if any) which might be necessary – i.e. *how* the person may come.

Friends in Meeting IX, looking at the procedure from the point of view of the about-to-be-released prisoner, say 'there may also be a value for the ex-offender in having this kind of "gateway", in that it may help to reinforce the reality of changes which are going to be necessary in day-to-day living in the future, as well as the necessary co-operation with the Probation Department.'

✳

South East Scotland Monthly Meeting have drawn up a document: *Notes for preparative meetings on responding to people who have abused children sexually* (see Appendix 2 for the full text). This makes the point that 'as meetings for worship are public, we have no legal right to bar anyone from attending, unless an injunction excluding an individual from a meeting has been obtained'. The document then sets out in detail measures which meetings may take to safeguard children, and at the same time deal humanely and in the spirit of Friends with those who have a conviction for abuse on their record.

South East Scotland Quakers suggest that this document might be used as a starting point by other meetings wishing to draw up their own guidelines.

✳

The benefit of having a procedure already in place was seen in Meeting X when a member, CD, was approached by an old friend soon to be released from prison and placed on the Sex Offenders' Register. He had visited Meeting X on a previous occasion and had therefore assumed that there would be no difficulty in his visiting once more. CD found it very helpful to be able to explain that the Quaker community had a procedure for such eventualities, that it was simple and confidential, starting with an approach to the Clerk. This, CD said, helped him out of a very embarrassing situation. There was something reassuring about having an administrative system to which a person could be referred.

Matters for Reflection

For the individual:

+ *What are my anxieties regarding the possibility of accepting into our meeting someone who has sexually abused others?*

For the group:

+ *Have we evaluated the risks involved in this matter? How far can we take risks on behalf of other people?*

+ *Where opinions differ, how far can we act in accordance with the teachings of Friends?*

9
Thinking about Trust

O f course, into the equation too comes trust, and this, given the present social climate, and the general feeling of nervousness, which a meeting may experience with regard to the whole issue of sexual offenders and safety, may be very difficult to foster.

Some Friends believe that Quaker meetings are based on trust freely offered, as a basic principle. In their view, asking all volunteers for work with children to apply for criminal records disclosure indicates mistrust and is therefore damaging to the sense of community. Others believe that when an abuser has broken trust, he must earn trust in future by a changed way of life. In addition, some people – not just Quakers – are wary of legal requirements and associated form-filling, distrusting the power of central government. Survivors observe any discussions keenly, gauging how much they could trust their meeting and the individuals in it. Trust enables people to live in society, feeling safe with most people most of the time.

Onora O'Neill in *A Question of Trust*, the 2002 Reith Lectures,[35] thinks that the claims by sociologists and journalists that we are 'in the grip of a deepening crisis of public trust that is directed even at our most familiar institutions and office holders' may not be completely valid. 'Loss of trust,' she says 'is the cliché of our times'. We may not be able to prove that there is a crisis of trust but we can certainly see 'massive evidence of a culture of suspicion'. On the other hand, observing how people behave shows that trust still exists significantly, in British society.

A Question of Trust is concerned with how this growing culture of suspicion is affecting people in public life. A new accountability has developed, one which demands an elaborate system of checks and balances. This is bringing about ever tighter administrative controls on institutional and professional life. However these developments are causing public cynicism and instead of encouraging us to trust public institutions they are damaging trust. There is no point either in trusting without reason. We need access to information and the means to make a balanced judgement

Onora O'Neill considers that 'deception is the real enemy of trust', and that 'deception lies at the heart of many serious crimes. If we want to increase trust we need to avoid *deception* rather than secrecy'. In public life moves which were intended to bring about transparency do in fact cause the reverse: the demand for transparency 'can encourage people to be less honest, so increasing deception and reducing reasons for trust'.

This, of course, is a general exploration of trust, in particular where public life is concerned, but it would seem to be important for us too in thinking of how we react to former sex offenders who might become part of our meeting. Blind trust in those who have previously offended is naïve, but constant suspicion will forever undermine their acceptance by the meeting and may elicit a very negative response from them too. We have to distinguish between someone being *trusted*, and someone being *trustworthy.*

We have to learn to trust the ways which have traditionally been used by Friends to address difficult matters. John Punshon describes the way decisions are made in meetings for business: 'What is required is a willingness to listen to what others have to say rather than to persuade them that one's own point of view represents what is right and proper. It also requires restraint . . . When conflict comes, as it does, and the temptation to compromise – to seek consensus – is resisted, the sense of divine guidance is unmistakably registered. New possibilities for a way forward, which nobody has thought of, emerge out of the discussion . . . Above all, those who take opposing views come to find that the discipline of waiting has mysteriously united them.'[36] The meeting could appoint a small clearness group to consider an issue in depth: see *Quaker faith & practice* 12.22–25.

We cannot offer a cast-iron guarantee of safety to those who are anxious at the idea of a former sex offender taking part in the meeting for worship and other activities. What we can say is that although bad things may happen, they will not destroy us. The Bible tells us many times 'Fear not, I am with you'. The medieval mystic Julian of Norwich reiterates this in the words frequently quoted from *Revelations of Divine Love*, 'sin is behovely, but all shall be well and all shall be well and all manner of thing shall be well'.[37]

Once we can see things clearly we are able to move from the darkness into the light. Strength should come to us from the voice of Isaac Penington, echoing down the years. The familiar opening phrases are comforting, the later lines recall the cruel realities of a violent community that was a gaol in the seventeenth century. From prison in 1667 he was able to write:

'Friends, Our life is love, and peace, and tenderness; and bearing one with another, and forgiving one another, and not laying accusations one against another; but praying one for another, and helping one another up with a tender hand, (if there has been any slip or fall); and waiting till the Lord gives sense and repentance, (if sense and repentance in any be wanting).

'Oh! Wait to feel this spirit, and to be guided. And then that which is contrary shall be trampled upon, as life rises and rules in you.

'So watch your hearts and ways; and watch one over another, in that which is gentle and tender, and knows it can neither preserve itself, nor help another out of the snare; but the Lord must be waited upon, to do this in and for us all.'

It is amazing that even from a prison cell Isaac Penington was able to continue exhorting Friends to live in the Light by taking care of one another. He tells us that we shall cope with whatever traumatic happenings may have befallen us – 'any thing that is, or hath been, or may be, amiss, ye will come over in the true dominion'. [38]

*

Meeting VIII has been considering the matter of trust with regard to allowing an ex-offender to be involved with children in his/her meeting. One of its members thinks that the Society's guidelines on child safety in meeting conflict with Quaker ethics, that is, the Christian principles of repentance and forgiveness, followed by the restoration of trust. Meeting VIII has drawn up several points from their discussion which have seemed important to them:

- We do not feel ourselves as having a role in forgiving or with-holding forgiveness (forgiving being a matter for the one who suffered from the offence and for God);
- We should be ready to be in full friendship with past offenders, being all past offenders in one way or another;
- While we do not at present have any alternative policy to offer, we do feel an outright ban in perpetuity would not really be in accordance with our belief in the possibility of change in a person and we do recognise that the Society's position is influenced by the current social context;
- We hope, therefore, that the subject will be revisited by Britain Yearly Meeting in a few years' time, to see whether our policy can properly be modified in any way.

*

In the end, without trust we are poor things. In order to 'live adventurously' we must trust. This trust is not a magic mantra which will secure us from all harm – no, it is rather an unshake-able faith that we will be upheld by divine guidance, so that come what may, we shall cope. We have to accept the fragility of human beings and rely upon the inner guide of whom George Fox spoke – we have to believe in 'that of God' within us because it is that which will give us the strength and the determination to win through fear and anxiety to the Light beyond.

Matters for Reflection

- *How can we create a climate of trust within the meeting?*
- *Is trust a gift, a right, a responsibility . . . ?*
- *In what ways can we learn to see 'that of God' in one another?*

10
Living in the Light

Reflection

In the introduction to *Advices and Queries* there is the postscript to an epistle to 'the brethren in the north' issued by a meeting of elders at Balby in 1656:

'Dearly beloved Friends, these things we do not lay upon you as a rule or form to walk by, but that all, with the measure of light which is pure and holy, may be guided; and so in the light walking and abiding, these may be fulfilled in the Spirit, not from the letter, for the letter killeth, but the Spirit giveth life.'[39]

George Fox and the early Friends speak of the 'Light' many times in their writings. They saw themselves as the Children of Light, their lives being illumined by the light of God, the power of which scorched them, revealing their failures and shortcomings. But by standing still and contemplating their weaknesses in the Light, they were reborn in the spirit.

Today we might wonder what this 'Light' might be – what is 'living in the Light'?

Light illuminates things, allows us to see them more clearly in their starkness – but something else must surely be present too, an added element – would we call it compassion, understanding, a being totally present in a situation?

George Fox writes in his *Journal* entry for 1647[40] of how God showed him his own sins and how from this darkness he emerged into the light:

'Yet I was under great temptations sometimes, and my inward sufferings were heavy; but I could find none to open my condition to but the Lord alone, unto whom I cried night and day. And I went back into Nottinghamshire, and there the Lord shewed me that the natures of those things which were hurtful without were within, in the hearts and minds of wicked men. The natures of dogs, swine, vipers, of Sodom and Egypt, Pharaoh, Cain, Ishmael, Esau etc. The natures I saw within, though people had been looking without. And I cried to the Lord saying, 'Why should I be thus, seeing I was never addicted to commit those evils?' And the Lord answered that it was needful I should have a sense of all conditions, how else should I speak to all conditions; and in this I saw the infinite love of God. I saw also that there was an ocean of darkness and death, but an infinite ocean of light and love, which flowed over the ocean of darkness. And in that also I saw the infinite love of God; and I had great openings.'

The founder of Quakerism was only 23: he had left home in some distress, wandering round the country, consulting famous preachers, spending time with some of the many independent religious groups that had sprung up in that time of civil and religious war. We do not nowadays understand some of Fox's vocabulary, though this figurative language was perfectly plain in the seventeenth century. In omitting the list of natures within, the 1995 publication *Quaker faith & practice* altered the significance of this passage.

Dogs were seen as willing to follow any strong leader, vipers were treacherous, Sodom and Egypt indicated all kinds of sexual and other perversions, Pharaoh signified a tyrannical nature, Cain murdered his own brother, Ishmael was an outsider, Esau betrayed his birthright for immediate gratification.

And swine? 'Applied opprobriously to sensual, degraded people who could lie with their own daughters':[41] incest and abuse, to be precise. Fox was desperate: he did not want these feelings, which he realised came from within and could not be blamed on outside pressures. He resisted behaving in those ways, why should have he have these urges? Truly, he was in an ocean of darkness.

It was only by confronting his own inner demons that George Fox was enabled to move beyond them into the Light and to receive the power which this gave him so that he was able to help others.

We have gradually been bringing hidden things into the light in recent years – we have witnessed this in the publication, as previously mentioned, of *Bringing the Invisible into the Light,* and in Friends' efforts to make us all aware of abusive situations, and in the need above all to protect children from hurt. This process is also making us look within ourselves at our own shortcomings. We have to recognise as George Fox did that we have the potential for 'all conditions'. If we indeed acknowledge this, we are less likely to project our fear and loathing of sexual abuse onto others. We will be more able to understand that given certain circumstances in a person's life someone may acquire distorted thinking. We will hate the actions caused by this, but will be enabled to look beyond these to the human being, and acknowledge his or her humanity.

In a passage written in 1648 George Fox speaks again about the transforming power of the inward Light: 'Now the Lord God hath opened to me by his invisible power how that every man was enlightened by the divine light of Christ; and I saw it shine through all, and that they that believed in it came out of condemnation and came to the light of life and became the children of light, but they that hated it, and did not believe in it, were condemned by it, though they made profession of Christ. This I saw in the pure openings of the Light without the help of any man, neither did I then know where to find it in the Scriptures; though after much searching I found it.'[42]

This revelation he tells us came to him directly and it was only later that he discovered confirmation of it set down in the Bible. George Fox and early Friends were 'fundamentalists' in that they went back to first sources. They gave their time, their attention, their commitment and their lives to the Light and so saw things unequivocally in a way many of us in the Society cannot today. Though we are living in fundamentalist times where people tend to look for neat, unambiguous answers to things, we as Quakers do not rely on a creed or a hierarchy but on being in touch with our inner life. We need to remember this when we are also dealing with so many situations in our daily life, including finding answers to healing the hurt in people's lives.

Harvey Gillman says that 'the spiritual journey is about how we are alive to one another'. He also tells us to 'listen to the sacred space of each other's experience'. [43]

The voices of early Friends ring with such passion and conviction that it is easy to see how they were able to endure persecution and imprisonment and continue unscathed in their faith. Their writings may also cause us to review what our own spiritual journey is and where it might be leading. Have we lost that zeal and passion of those early Friends? Can we translate it to our own times?

Spiritual practice

In the letter to Lady Claypole in 1658 George Fox[44] is trying to console Oliver Cromwell's favourite daughter who was very depressed following the death of her child, and seriously ill (she would herself die in a few months). She was also faced with the knowledge that her father, the Protector, had lost the trust of the people, and was near death too. Fox tells her to 'be still and cool in thy own mind and spirit from thy own thoughts, and then thou wilt feel the principle of God to turn thy mind to the Lord God, whereby thou wilt receive his strength and power from whence life comes, to allay all tempests, against blusterings and storms'. Fox continues throughout the letter telling her to trust in God, and that this will sustain her through out her trials. Could this spiritual practice be helpful to a survivor? Not if it is suggested as a quick answer to the hurt caused by abuse, or a religious duty – but when the time is right, when the survivor is ready, 'turning thy mind to God' will bring clearness and strength.

Rex Ambler, in studying George Fox's central message encapsulated in his writings about the Inward Light, has deduced that early Friends practised a form of meditation, a discipline, where they focused on the illuminating spirit within them.

In *Light to Live By* Rex Ambler transcribes George Fox's texts into modern idiom so that we can more easily understand his message. He also sets out a meditation guide for workshops and 'Light Groups' to enable us to live in the Light ourselves.

George Fox was saying essentially that we may be freed by the truth, and that we are all able to find this truth if we look within ourselves and allow the Inward Light, the Light of God, to illuminate our being. Only by daring to turn inwards and looking unflinchingly at what lies there, can we achieve this. Preachers, doctrines, rituals, none of these can set us free: the responsibility and the challenge lie with us alone. We may have to work through guilt and shame to find the truth about ourselves. Margaret Fell warned that 'the Light will rip you open.'[45] Nevertheless at the same time that we see the truth about ourselves we also see the mercy of God and find forgiveness.

Rex Ambler describes the process:

'We have three steps here:
1. See yourselves in the Light,
2. Stand still in the Light,
3. Submit to the Light.

'Then mercy comes and power and strength, but these don't count as "steps" because they come as a gift. They are not human actions. The human action in the process is surprisingly non-active, though: see, stand still, submit. To these three we need to add a fourth, which is the step that gets the process going and it is always Fox's first advice: Mind the Light, i.e. pay attention to it.'[46]

A number of Light Groups have been set up in several meetings, to practise this spiritual discipline together. In such groups people are able to share their innermost feelings; they learn to 'know one another in the things which are eternal'. [47] Sensitivity is needed, though, in discerning when to offer such an opportunity. Participants should know, too, that pastoral care is available.

If meetings and individuals had the courage to venture into this new territory, it is possible that those with past hurts might find relief through the sharing of them. Maybe those who have done the hurting will change, when they too 'stand still in the Light'. It is significant that the process of reaching the Light should start with a silence, a waiting, and through the standing still the centring may come and then the illumination. Fear leaves us when we confront it. Sometimes in worship or in our communities it would appear that people fail to be honest with one another because they do not know how others will react to the truth. If we try really to 'live in the Light' we will liberate both ourselves and others and create an environment where difficult things may be approached with tenderness and love.

An awareness of the crucial nature of the Light has also been expressed by many other contemporary Friends. Ursula Franklin in 1979 wrote that 'I have never lost the enjoyment of sitting in silence at the beginning of meeting, knowing that everything can happen, knowing the joy of utmost surprise, feeling that nothing is preordained, nothing is set, all is open. The light can come from all sides. The joy of experiencing the Light in a completely different way than one has thought it would come is one of the greatest gifts that Friends' meeting for worship has brought me.' [48]

The knowledge of this transforming Light removes all barriers between people, as Meg Maslin found: 'Guided by the Light of God within us and recognising that of God in others, we can all learn to value our differences in age sex, physique, race and culture.' [49]

Clearness meetings [50] may also help us to work through difficulties and discord to reach the light and the source of worship. These are ways of sorting things out, finding the way forward and creating harmony. But above all, we need to be honest with one another – where information is withheld and people do not really know what is happening, suspicion and fear can thrive. We can neither trust, nor live in the Light if we are being dishonest with one another.

George Fox said, shortly before his death 'I am glad I was here. Now I am clear, I am fully clear. All is well; the Seed of God reigns over all and over death itself. And though I am weak in body, yet the power of God is over all, and the Seed reigns over all disorderly spirits.' [51] He was able to say this because he felt he had sorted out his life and was ready to die. This surely is how we would all most like to feel at the end of our lives: that we had worked through difficulties and trials, enjoyed the journey but are now at peace and prepared for death.

In the matter of how we as Friends rise to the challenge posed by the potential presence of sex offenders in our meetings it becomes very apparent that if we are to reach wise decisions, we need to rely above all on the Inward Light. Surely Quaker teaching with its stress on witnessing to the truth will help us to devise imaginative ways which will heal both the abused and the abuser. We are living in times when many people despair because they have lost the ability to trust. People, individuals, may be untrustworthy in some way. Friends have trusted in the Inward Light for over three hundred years and it has never failed. We have to hold this belief steady in our hearts and go forward in faith.

Matters for Reflection

+ *How much illumination can I bear in my life?*
+ *How can I use my beliefs as a Friend to help me reach the Light on this issue?*
+ *What spiritual practices have I found helpful?*

11
Last Thoughts

These pages have enabled people to express their personal anguish.

We have heard the testimony of those struggling to free themselves from years of secret hurt, the brave stories of coming to terms and finding a sort of peace.

Ex-offenders have told of their broken lives and of their remorse, of their being stranded in limbo but hoping for acceptance somewhere.

Then there are the stories of parents fearful for their children's safety, the disillusionment, anger, and feelings of betrayal where those looking after their children prove to be abusers too. Trust has been undermined and there has been some confusion.

Meetings have debated how to act, and people have been shocked by the depth of feeling which has been aroused.

So what has emerged from all this? At first it might appear that meetings have often been polarised in their response, with some putting the ex-prisoners' viewpoint and others stressing that the safety of children and the need to protect vulnerable adults is paramount. But surely these two 'positions' are much closer than we would imagine – in fact they merge – they are sides of the same coin.

As we know, many abusers have themselves been abused; they are also victims – this has been starkly brought out in the words of Marian Partington when she realised that her sister's abuser and killer had herself suffered a life of appalling abuse. Knowing this we need to ensure two things. We must keep today's children free from harm by being vigilant and by putting safeguards in place. Secondly, we need to adopt a flexible approach to those of us who are ex-offenders. With some thought everyone can be accommodated in our meetings. It is only by helping those who have offended to be integrated safely into the community, that we can be of benefit both to our children and also to the ex-offenders. When people feel polarised they react negatively. People who feel safe and accepted can spread their joy about them.

At the same time as we recognise the interconnectedness of survivors and offenders, we must also never forget that faith communities tend to attract abusers. And perhaps even more vital: most sex offences occur in families and with family friends.

This is not to end on a note of doom and gloom, it is rather to take a realistic view of the situation. We have brought suffering into the light and this surely is positive because it relieves the oppressed and it shows us the truth. Query 37 (quoted previously, on page 3), asking us whether we are 'honest in word and deed', should help us ensure, if we live by it, that we are working towards a better world where real transparency informs people's actions.

The writing of these pages has been very difficult because of the need to do justice to the suffering of the injured – probably only a person who has suffered sexual abuse can appreciate the full extent of the trauma which it creates in people's lives. We could weep at the thought of young lives twisted and scarred. Beside these are the stories of parents betrayed and confused.

Those reading this book will no doubt interpret it in different ways, but suffice it to say that all these stories are really part of the same fabric and in the end indivisible.

*

Watch your hearts and ways; and watch one over another, in that which is gentle and tender, and knows it can neither preserve itself, nor help another out of the snare; but the Lord must be waited upon, to do this in and for us all. (Isaac Penington)[38]

Sources
of quotations and books referred to in the text

1   *Grounded in God*, Ed. Patricia McBee, Quaker Press of Friends General Conference, 2002, pp 211–212

2   *Quaker faith & practice* 19.32. This book (*Qfp*) is the book of Christian discipline of the Yearly Meeting of the Religious Society of Friends (Quakers) in Britain, published in 1995. This anthology of inspirational passages and guidance on church government is the authoritative book about Quakers in Britain

3   *Qfp* 1.02.37

4   *Qfp* 19.07, Margaret Fell quoting George Fox

5   *Qfp* 19.46, Margaret Fell's paper to Parliament, one of the earliest of Quaker statements on peace

6   *Qfp* 1.18

7   John Lampen, *Mending Hurts* 1987, p 15

8   *Qfp* 21.66

9   *Qfp* 19.03, George Fox in his journal, 1647

10 Marian Partington, *Salvaging the Sacred: Lucy, my sister*, Quaker Books, 2004

11 Alison Leonard, *Living in Godless Times: tales of spiritual travellers*, Floris Books 2001, p 127

12 Lesley Moreland, *An Ordinary* Murder, Aurum Press, 2001

13 Tim Newell, *Forgiving Justice*, QHS, 2000 (Swarthmore Lecture), p 71

14 Marian Liebmann, in *Restorative Justice – what's it all about?* CTBI, p 6

15 Rupert Ross, *Returning to the Teachings, exploring aboriginal justice*, Penguin Books, 1996, p 65

16 Quaker Women's Group, *Bringing the Invisible into the Light: some Quaker feminists speak of their experience*, Quaker Home Service, 1986 (Swarthmore Lecture)

17 *Bringing the Invisible into the Light*, p 46

18 Hazel Shellens, 'We shall forever eat frugally off clean plates: an analysis of the background, presentation and effect of the 1986 Swarthmore Lecture,' unpublished M.Phil thesis submitted to the University of Birmingham; published version *Was the Invisible Brought into the Light? The 1986 Quaker Women's Group Swarthmore Lecture*, Birmingham: Woodbrooke Quaker Study Centre, 2004

19 *We shall forever . . . .* , p 32

20 Judy L. Brutz, *Parable and Transforming Power among Friends: an address given to Illinois and Ohio Valley Yearly Meetings*, Illinois Publications committee 1986, p 1

21 E. Hardisty, C. Cannon and R. Turner, *What can we say about child sexual abuse?* Chester Preparative Meeting, 1997

22 *Safeguarding Children from Harm*, Quaker Home Service, 1996: the Children Act 1989 interpreted for Quaker meetings

23 *Health, Safety and the Law*, Quaker Home Service, 1991

24 *Meeting Safety*, Quaker Home Service, 2001

25 Kate Cairns *Surviving Paedophilia: traumatic stress after organised and network child sexual abuse*, Trentham Books, 1999

26 See the Supplement to *Meeting Safety* on working with the Criminal Records Bureau

27 *Qfp* 19.32, George Fox's letter to a minister in 1656, written from prison

28 Roger Hood, Stephen Shute, Martina Feilzer, Aidan Wilcox, 'Reconviction rates of serious sex offenders and assessment of their risk', *Home Office Findings* No 164, 2002

29 *Qfp* 1.01, from a postscript to a letter of advice from elders, 1656, quoting Paul's letter to Corinthians, II 3:6

30 John Lampen, *Mending Hurts*, Quaker Home Service, 1987, p 61

31 *Community Reintegration Project: Circles of Support and Accountability*, Revised edition 2000, p 10 – originally published by the Mennonite Central Committee, Spring 1996

32 *Qfp*, 1.01, the preamble to the *Advices and Queries*

33 *Qfp* 1.02.18

34 *Qfp* 23.98, quoting from Elizabeth Fry, *Observations on the visiting of female prisoners,* 1827, pp 21–22

35 Onora O'Neill, *A Question of Trust*, Cambridge University Press, 2002: the book of the Reith Lectures, BBC Radio 4, 2002, pp 18–19

36 *Qfp*, 2.90, quoting from John Punshon, *Encounter with Silence: reflections from the Quaker tradition*, 1987, p 98

37 Julian of Norwich, *Revelations of Divine Love*

38 *Works of Isaac Penington*, Vol IV, Quaker Heritage Press, 1995, letter shortened. The opening sentence can be found in *Qfp* 10.01

39 *Qfp* 1.01

40 George Fox, *Journal*, ed. J.L. Nickalls, 1952, pp 2–3. This passage is also quoted in *Qfp*, 19.03, but the list of 'the natures' is omitted

41 Oxford *New English Dictionary*: '*swine* applied opprobriously to a sensual, degraded or coarse person' with early quotation from 1430 'How that this swyn . . . lay bi his douhter . . .'

42 *Qfp* 19.04

43 Harvey Gillman in a public talk to a meeting of Quakers in Hull on 25th July 2002 entitled 'Communicating the Spiritual Quest in a puzzled world'

44 George Fox, *Journal* pp 346–348, where the whole letter may be found; quoted in part in *Qfp* 2.18

45 Margaret Fell, *An Epistle to Convinced Friends*, 1656, in *Margaret Fell Speaking*, ed. Hugh Barbour, Pendle Hill Pamphlet #206

46 Rex Ambler *Light to Live By: an exploration in Quaker spirituality* Quaker Books, 2002, p 45

47 *Advices and queries* 18

48 *Qfp* 23.32

49 *Qfp* 23.33

50 See for example, *Qfp* 12.22–25

51 *Qfp* 21.49

Appendix 1
Words and definitions

Advices and queries chapter one of *Quaker faith & practice* (see below), used for reflection and meditation, and much loved by all Quakers. It can also be read as summary of Quaker faith.

Alternatives to Violence Project (AVP) a programme, developed by Quakers but now independent, to help people in prison deal constructively with aggression.

Attender an attender is a person who attends a Quaker meeting for worship regularly, but who is not in membership of the Religious Society of Friends.

Birthright Friend until 1960 the children of Quaker parents automatically became members at birth. These Friends are referred to as 'birthright Friends'.

Britain Yearly Meeting short for the 'Yearly Meeting of the Religious Society of Friends (Quakers) in Britain', the formal name of the British Quakers as a church.

Convincement, Friends by those who have become members of the Society through their own convictions, as young people or adults, rather than by right of birth (pre-1960) or application of their parents on their behalf.

Elder elders are appointed to take a special responsibility for the spiritual welfare of the meeting as a community and of all the individual worshippers, whether in formal membership or attending regularly. In a tenth of meetings, approximately, the work of eldership is shared by all the worshippers, and 'elder' then refers to someone who is, at that particular moment, carrying out one of the tasks of eldership.

Friend among themselves, Quakers call each other 'Friend': this recalls the early name for the Society, 'Friends of Truth', and emphasises both the equality between and the care for each worshipper, whether young or old, whatever their marital status, race or culture, social class or profession, or their office in the Society.

Light, usually 'inward' or 'inner' Light The Inward Light is the light of Christ. It is a universal Light, which can be known by anyone, of either sex, of any age, of whatever religions. The experience of the Light is fundamental to Friends and to their theology. See also 'that of God' below.

Meeting The name for the most essential and characteristic activity of Quakers, the meeting for worship (also meeting for marriage, for burial, for business, etc, all held in worship), and also the name for the units in the structure, e.g. yearly meeting, monthly (or area) meeting, preparative (or local) meeting.

Meeting house many Quaker meetings own a building where they meet for worship. The meeting room is not consecrated: it will be plainly furnished, without an altar or any religious decoration, the seating often in a circle so all can see the other worshippers, and no seats of different status. Meeting houses are often used by local charities, playgroups and other community groups.

Meeting for worship Quakers meet in silent waiting, open together to God's Light and inward communion. A few individuals may speak, to share some insight of the Spirit. It is not group meditation; there is no liturgy, no priest, no bread and wide, no religious artefacts. The elders appointed for the day will make arrangements (heating on, chairs set out, etc.) and close the meeting by shaking hands.

Overseer Overseers are appointed to take a special responsibility for aspects of pastoral care within the meeting. In a tenth of meetings, approximately, the work of oversight is shared by all the worshippers, and 'overseer' then refers to someone who is, at that particular moment, carrying out one of the tasks of oversight.

Preparative meeting see meeting, above.

Prison minister the Quaker appointed to serve on a prison chaplaincy team.

Quaker an early nickname, now the name we are mostly known by.

Quaker faith and practice the anthology of inspiration, advice and guidance for Quakers in Britain, revised every generation, also known as 'the book of Christian discipline'. The 1995 edition is the authoritative book about British Quaker theology and structure today. Often abbreviated to *Qfp* in writing, to 'faith and practice' in conversation.

Schedule 1 sexual offence see page 2 for full explanation

Swarthmore Lecture lectures, with accompanying books, presented to Yearly Meeting since 1907, offering significant contributions to Quaker theology, practice and faith.

That of God in every one another expression (see Light, above) of Quaker experience, the belief that each person has a potential for goodness, a conscience and a yearning for the divine which can be addressed and evoked, or repressed, damaged or in some people almost destroyed.

Appendix 2

The experience of South East Scotland

South East Scotland Monthly Meeting

Notes for Preparative Meetings on responding to people who have abused children sexually. Approved by South East Scotland MM, Minute 3.05 of 2002.

1. Some people who have been convicted of, or are suspected of having committed, sexual offences against children, wish to attend Quaker meetings for worship and other meeting activities. The booklets *Meeting Safety* (Quaker Home Service) and *Guidance to Churches: Protecting Children and Appointing Children's Workers* (Churches' Child Protection Advisory Service) offer guidance on how to respond to this challenge. The *Child Protection Guidelines* drawn up by your local authority should be followed.

2. As meetings for worship are public, we have no legal right to bar anyone from attending, unless an injunction excluding an individual from the Meeting House has been obtained. In order to do this, it is necessary to prove that there are reasonable grounds for suspecting that the named person will offend on the premises. Friends will wish to welcome all individuals, whatever their background, within guidelines laid down to ensure the safety of the children associated with meetings. However, specific issues have to be addressed concerning the possibility of meetings being approached by people who have abused children sexually.

3. The underlying philosophy of *Meeting Safety* is that we seek to respond to that of God in everyone, while remembering our prime responsibility for the well being of children and young people. The implications of people who have been convicted (or who say they are at risk) of committing sexual offences against children attending meeting need to be discussed by Elders and Overseers, members of Children's Committee, and Preparative meeting.

4. We need to consider both the risks posed by someone who has offended in this way, and the measures required to contain these risks. Assessment of the risk of further offending is difficult. Some individuals are unlikely to offend again and may be profoundly repentant. At the opposite end of a spectrum are others with compulsive criminal behaviour, which they fail to admit or see as harmful. Containment

may also be difficult. For example, contact between children and an offender may be successfully prevented within a Meeting House; however, children might see respected adults talking to a visitor/ Attender at the end of meeting and assume, should they encounter the visitor/ Attender elsewhere, that the person can be fully trusted. When a child is approached by somebody intent on offending (whether or not this person is known to parents or members of a meeting), the child's safety will depend largely on how she or he responds to the individual. It is therefore very important that those responsible for children in meeting consider with parents how to prepare children for such encounters.

5. A person who has abused children sexually must never be involved in work with children or young people in any context and must never be permitted to be alone with children or young people. Where an offer of service with children has to be refused due to application of this rule, and indeed in all dealings with people who have offended, the individual needs the loving support of the meeting.

6. It is very helpful if clear boundaries can be agreed in writing with the offender. The agreement, which will need to be reviewed regularly, should be signed by the individual and a designated person, who both keep copies. It should stipulate which people designated by the meeting will be given personal information about the individual, and will include an undertaking that they will treat this information as confidential. If the offender is subject to statutory supervision, it may be helpful to include the criminal justice social worker (in England and Wales, the probation officer) in the agreement. Compliance with the boundaries requires monitoring, and if necessary enforcement. If the meeting does not feel that it can, for the time being, provide adequate protection for its children if the offender attends the regular meetings for worship, can he or she be offered worship with a group of adults from this or another Preparative meeting?

7. It is important to observe the distinction between consideration of the topic in a general manner by members of the meeting, and disclosure of information concerning an individual. The latter must be on a need-to-know basis. With a person's consent, a small number (four or less) of designated people in the meeting, one of whom should act as co-ordinator, will need sufficient information about an offender's history to meet their responsibility to the meeting. Only these people should know the identity of the person. They should be responsible for a rota to look out for, and keep an eye on, the offender whenever

there is a meeting for Worship, or other activity open to all who worship with us. Their identity is best not disclosed as this could lead to identification of the offender. They must be chosen with care and their work needs to be upheld by the meeting. They may also require professional care and support.

8. Information about the offender must only be given to designated people who can be trusted to keep it confidential. Inappropriate disclosure has the potential to cause much anxiety and suffering. It may incur acts of hostility towards the individual, members of the meeting, or meeting premises. It may also attract unwelcome attention from members of the public and media, leading possibly to an offender having to move out of the area. Elders might consider how they would respond to a reporter asking why the meeting had welcomed a sex offender. The name of an offender cannot be disclosed to anyone without the informed consent of the person, preferably in writing. Inappropriate disclosure of information infringes the right to privacy of an individual who could then sue the meeting or members of the meeting.

9. When a sex offender against children wishes to attend meeting, one of the designated members of the meeting should contact the relevant after-care agencies, particularly the local criminal justice social work department, and ascertain any legal restrictions placed on the individual. The department should be asked to corroborate the offender's self report of his or her behaviour, but is likely to do this only with the offender's permission. If this cannot be obtained, it may be necessary to ask advice of the Sex Offender Liaison Officer (who is a police officer or social worker, or in Wales and England a probation officer). People who have not offended but have disclosed an urge to do so may present a high risk. The best course is to encourage such people to consult their doctor, who can arrange expert help. If the nature of past offences, or possible offences, is unclear, advice should be sought from the police or social work department.

10. Though members of Monthly Meeting are not aware that any cases of sexual abuse to children have occurred as a result of offenders attending Quaker meetings, we need to be alert to the possibility of this occurring in the future, and to remember that the risk is not confined to people, who are known to have committed offences in the past. [see note below**]

11. Concerning transfer of any Friend between meetings, *Quaker faith and practice* (11.31) advises that: 'It may be desirable that the Overseers of the meeting from which the Friend is moving write to the Clerk

to Overseers of the receiving meeting giving such information in confidence as may be felt to be useful.' In the same way, it is important for information to be passed on confidentially about a person, who has offended sexually against children, who is known to members of one meeting, if the person is likely to attend another meeting.

12. Decisions about attendance at Quaker meetings, or meeting functions, by people who have offended sexually against children need prayerful consideration. Though the responsibility is considerable, wise handling of the issue can bring deep satisfaction. The success of the Circles of Support and Accountability programme for sex offenders suggests appropriate support by members of meeting and others could reduce the likelihood of re-offending. Friends might consider recording the non-minuted aspects of their own meeting's process, as such records could be of help to other meetings.

** *Note from the editors:* sexual abuse of children and adults has occurred under the shelter of local Quaker communities within this and other Yearly Meetings, which confirms the point made in section 10, above.

Appendix 3
Resources: Publications

This list includes those books quoted in the text, and also some other books that have been annotated as offering various kinds of help to readers. Contact the Quaker Bookshop for purchases, or the Quaker Life Resources Room to borrow (see Appendix 4 for contact details).

Ambler, Rex, *A Light to Live By: an exploration in Quaker Spirituality*, Quaker Books 2002.

Bass, Ellyn and Davis, Laura, *The Courage to Heal*, Cedar 1991
Explores all aspects of recovery, with exercises and ideas for resolving difficulties. Written mainly for women, but the latest edition includes male experiences.

Bringing the Invisible into the Light, see Quaker Women's Group.

Brutz, Judy L., *Parable and Transforming power among Friends: an address given to Illinois and Ohio Valley Yearly Meetings*, Illinois Publications Committee 1986.

Cairns, Kate, *Surviving Paedophilia: traumatic stress after organised and network child sexual abuse* Trentham Books, 1999.

Cashman, Hilary, *Christianity and child sexual abuse*, SPCK 1993.
Trying to understand how churches, including Quaker meetings, have failed to meet the needs of victims and abusers, beginning to stand alongside those who are suffering or threatened, or shadowed by memory.

Davis, Laura, *The Courage to Heal Workbook: for women and men survivors of child sexual assault*, Harper Collins, 1990 (out of print in UK but available from US, eg through www.amazon.co.uk).
Companion to Bass and Davis *The Courage to Heal*: provides an explanation of the healing process, first-person accounts of recovery, and practical suggestions. The book also contains insights and strategies for partners and counsellors of survivors.

Eldership & Oversight, Committee on, *Conflict in Meetings*, Quaker Home Service, 2000.

Eldership & Oversight, Committee on, *Pastoral Care of Children and Young People*, Quaker Home Service, 2000.
Includes consideration of special overseers for the young.

Eldership & Oversight, Committee on, *A Delicate Balance*, and *Sexual Harassment*.
Leaflets on dealing with sexual harassment; texts can be downloaded from the BYM website: www.quaker.org.uk

Elliott, Michele, *Be Smart, Stay Safe: The Willow Street Kids*, Pan Macmillan 1997.
What would you do if someone tried to bully you? An older person tried to touch you in a way that made you feel uncomfortable? The Willow Street Kids know how to Be Smart and Stay Safe: true stories of their adventures and dilemmas for ages 7 to 11.

Elliott, Michele, *Feeling Happy, Feeling Safe: a Safety Guide for Young Children*, Hodder Children's books, 1991 (out of print, can be borrowed from Quaker Life Resources Room).
Illustrated story book for reading with children under 6, to help them learn how to deal with unpleasant experiences including potential abuse.

Facing the Unthinkable: protecting children from abuse, Churches' Child Protection Advisory Service, 1998.
A video workpack, with leaders' notes, practical exercises and photocopiable take-home information for participants.

Fell, Margaret, ed. Hugh Barbour, *Margaret Fell Speaking*, Wallingford, Pennsylvania: Pendle Hill, 1976 (Pendle Hill Pamphlet #206).

Fox, George, ed. J.L. Nickalls, *Journal*, Quaker Home Service and Pennsylvania YM, 1997 (original publication London Yearly Meeting, 1952).

Guidance to Churches: protecting children and appointing children's workers, plus policy documents disc. Churches Child Protection Advisory Service.
A comprehensive guide, updates can be downloaded from the CCPAS website (see Appendix 4, Organisations).

Grounds for optimism with Personality Disorders, James Nayler Foundation proceedings of Annual Conference 2001

Hardisty, E., Cannon, C., and Turner, R. *What can we say about child sexual abuse?* Chester Preparative Meeting, 1997.

Health, Safety and the Law, see *Meeting Safety*

Hood, R., Shute, S., Feilzer, M., Wilcox, A., 'Reconviction rates of serious sex offenders and assessment of their risk', *Home Office Findings No 164*, 2002

Julian of Norwich, *Revelations of Divine Love*, many versions in modern English available, e.g. published by Penguin.

Kennedy, Margaret, *The Courage to Tell: Christian Survivors of sexual abuse tell their stories.* Churches Together in Britain and Ireland, 1999.
Adult survivors' stories, illustrated by squares from a wall-hanging, embroidered by contributors to help express their feelings.

Lampen, John, *Mending Hurts*, Quaker Home Service, 1987 (Swarthmore Lecture).
From experience with young offenders, and in Northern Ireland.

Leonard, Alison, *Living in Godless Times: tales of spiritual travellers*, Floris Books, 2001.
Based on extended interviews, including some Quakers.

MacLeod, Mary, *Child protection: everybody's business*, Childline, 1997.
Study as part of a joint campaign by *Community Care* and Childline, throwing light on dilemmas facing friends, neighbours, relatives, teachers and others worried about a child. Highlights concerns and experiences of the child protection system, and draws out lessons for policy-makers, managers, practitioners and any adults concerned about children's safety.

McBee, Patricia (ed.), *Grounded in God*, Quaker Press of Friends General Conference, 2002.
Collected articles on pastoral care in Quaker meetings, including responding to abuse, people with mental illness and conflict in meetings. Advice based on experience, plus questions for reflection,

thus suitable for training in oversight.

Meeting Safety: a code of good practice with comprehensive guidance for volunteers working on children and young people's activities and Quaker events, Quaker Home Service, 2001, with supplement: *Procedures for working with the Criminal Records Bureau*.
Guidelines on health, safety and well-being of young people, children and the adults who work with them, drawing on the experience of local Quaker meetings in Britain. Supersedes *Safeguarding Children from Harm*, and *Health, safety and the law*.

Meeting the Challenge: how churches should respond to sex offenders, Church of England, 1999.
Good brief theological exploration, but reflects the legislation in force at that time. See *Protecting . . .* , below.

Mennonite Central Committee, *Community Reintegration Project: Circles of Support and Accountability*, Toronto 1996, 2000

Methodist Church, *The Church and Sex Offenders: Report to conference 2000*, Methodist Publishing House, 2000

Moreland, Lesley, *An Ordinary Murder*, Aurum Press, 2001.

Newell, Tim, *Forgiving Justice*, Quaker Home Service, 2000 (Swarthmore Lecture).

O'Neill, Onora, *A Question of Trust*, Cambridge University Press, 2002.

Partington, Marian, *Salvaging the Sacred: Lucy, my sister*, Quaker Books, 2004.

Pellauer, M.D., Chester, B., Boyajian, J. *Sexual Assault and Abuse: a handbook for clergy and religious professionals*, Harper San Francisco, 1987.
Twenty essays exploring theology and other aspects, a useful start to considering how religion and abuse inter-relate.

Penington, Isaac, *Works*, Quaker Heritage Press, 1995.

Poling, James Newton, *The Abuse of Power*, Abingdon Press, 1991.
Exploring theology, psychology, politics and our culture which sanctions male dominance: difficult reading, but confronts assumptions but offers a healing theology too.

Protecting all God's children: the child protection policy for the Church of England, Church House Publishing, 3rd edition 2004.
Helpfully considers ministering to people who might pose a risk to children.

Quaker faith and practice: the book of Christian discipline of the Yearly Meeting of the Religious Society of Friends (Quakers) in Britain. Britain Yearly Meeting, 1995.

Quaker Women's Group, *Bringing the Invisible into the Light*, Quaker Home Service 1986 (Swarthmore Lecture).

Restorative Justice: what's it all about? Papers in advance of a conference, organised by the Churches' Criminal Justice Forum of Churches Together in Britain and Ireland, 2001.

Ross, Rupert, *Returning to the Teachings, exploring Aboriginal Justice*, Penguin Books, Canada, 1996.

Safeguarding Children from Harm, see *Meeting Safety*

Shellens, Hazel, 'We shall forever eat frugally off clean plates: an analysis of the background, presentation and effect of the 1986 Swarthmore Lecture,' unpublished M.Phil thesis submitted to the University of Birmingham; published version *Was the Invisible Brought into the Light? The 1986 Quaker Women's Group Swarthmore Lecture*, Birmingham: Woodbrooke Quaker Study Centre, 2004

Skidmore, C. & G. (eds.), *Beyond My Control: Quakers talk about their personal experience of addiction*, The Sowle Press, Reading, 2002

Stott, Sarah, *Out of the Shadows: help for men who have been sexually assaulted*, Russell House, 2001.
Designed to empower survivors, challenge the secrecy and silence about the sexual assault of men and boys, and help workers who seek to support them. Written straightforwardly, describing the effect abuse may have, and ways survivors can address the practical and emotional issues.

Time for Action: sexual abuse, the Churches and a new dawn for survivors, Churches Together in Britain and Ireland, 2002.
Challenges all religious groups to really listen to those who have been sexually abused and to provide appropriate pastoral care. Addresses the protection of children and adults and how a church may cope with incorporating into its community a known abuser.

Wyre, Ray, and Swift, Anthony, *Women, Men and Rape*, Hodder and Stoughton, 1990 (now only available in booklet form, from Ray Wyre Associates, 01908 225540, www.sexualcrime.com).
A well documented analysis. With women readers primarily in mind, discusses the psychology of the rapist and sexual attacker, and the attitudes of society and the legal system to offender and victim. Interviews with offenders offer disturbing insights. Strongly argues for a fundamentally new approach to the deterrence of rape. Similar considerations of child abuse and obscene phone calls included.

Appendix 4
Resources: Organisations

This can only be a short list, but it is a starting point. In our experience the staff answering calls at these organisations can refer enquiries to more appropriate or relevant organisations. The contact details were correct at the end of 2003. The books in Appendix 3 often list more organisations, too.

Quaker committees and staff support

Those listed below can all be contacted by post, or in person during working hours at the central offices of the Quakers
- Friends House, 173–177 Euston Road, London NW1 2BJ, England
- telephone for general enquiries: 020 7663 1000

Website of Britain Yearly Meeting – with links to many Quaker and other relevant sites
- www.quaker.org.uk

Children & Young People's Section – for advice on protection, spiritual nurture and pastoral care of children and young people
- The Secretary – direct telephone: 020 7663 1013, e-mail: janetf@quaker.org.uk

The Quaker Bookshop
- direct telephone: 020 7663 1030
- e-mail: bookshop@quaker.org.uk
- for secure online shopping go to: www.quaker.org.uk/bookshop

Committee on Eldership & Oversight – which is exploring how those locally responsible for oversight and eldership can respond supportively to survivors of abuse in their meetings
- The Secretary – direct telephone: 020 7662 1023, e-mail anneh@quaker.org.uk

The Reference Group (Criminal Records) and *Quaker Approvals Group (Criminal Records)* – for advice on criminal records bureau procedures and how sex offenders can be welcomed safely to Quaker meetings
- The Secretary, direct telephone: 020 7663 1023, e-mail anneh@quaker.org.uk

The Quaker Life Resources Room – for borrowing books and other resources by post or in person
- direct telephone: 020 7663 1023
- e-mail: ql@quaker.org.uk

Quaker Peace and Social Witness, Information Officer – for information about Circles of Support and Accountability
- telephone: 020 7663 1000
- e-mail: qpsw@quaker.org.uk

Other organizations

Local authority child protection unit, criminal justice social work department (in Scotland) or probation service (in England and Wales). Start by looking in your local telephone book for your local authority (look for the Social Services or Child Protection department), or under Probation Service.

Quaker Women Survivors of Childhood Sexual Abuse
- contact Bunty Walsh on telephone: 01480 413413 or e-mail: bunty. walsh@ntlworld.com

The National Association for People Abused in Childhood (NAPAC)
- 42 Curtain Road, London EC2A 3NH
- 020 8971 5099
- e-mail: mail@napac.fsnet.co.uk
- freephone helpline Mon to Fri 12.00 to 8.00pm and Sat 9.00am to 12.00: 0800 085 3330

Childline – for children in trouble or danger
- Freepost 1111, London N1 0BR
- freephone helpline: 0800 1111
- web-site: www.childline.org.uk

One in Four – run for and by people who have experienced sexual abuse
- 219 Bromley Road, London SE6 2PG
- telephone: 020 8697 2112
- e-mail: support@oneinfour.org
- web-site: www.oneinfour.org.uk

Christian Survivors of Sexual Abuse (CSSA) – for Christian adults sexually abused in childhood.
- BM-CSSA, London WC1N 3XX

Churches' Child Protection Advisory Service – an independent Christian charity providing professional child protection advice and support to churches and organisations
- P. O. BOX 133, Swanley, Kent BR8 7UQ
- helpline: 0845 120 4551
- web-site: www.ccpas.co.uk

Relate – offers a range of relationship support services. Many branches run support groups for survivors, and counselling if abuse issues are affecting your relationship
- helpline open Monday to Friday, 9.30 to 4.30: 0845 130 40 10.
- web-site: www.relate.org.uk
- for your local number, see telephone directory

Survivors UK – if you want to find out more about individual counselling, facilitated groups, training and the National Register of Male Sexual Assault Counsellors.
- helpline Tues and Thurs 7pm to 10pm: 020 7357 6677
- web-site: www.survivorsuk.co.uk

Kidscape – helps parents keep children safe.
- Grosvenor Gardens, London sw1w 0DH
- telephone: 020 7730 3300
- e-mail: www.kidscape.org.uk

Stop It Now! UK – provides information and help for all adults, including abusers and potential abusers, to protect children from abuse.
- P. O. BOX 9841, Birmingham B48 7BW
- telephone: 01527 598 184, freephone helpline 0808 1000 900
- web-site: www.stopitnow.org.uk